A BIRDWATCHER'S QUIZ BOOK

By the same author:
Evenings at the Coot and Corncrake (Collins 1986)

A BIRD-WATCHER'S QUIZ BOOK

COMPILED BY

Chris Harbard

FOREWORD BY

Magnus Magnusson

CARTOONS BY

Philip Snow

MISLEADING NOTEBOOKS BY

Crispin Fisher

COLLINS
8 Grafton Street London W1

First Published by William Collins Sons & Co Ltd 1987

Planned and Produced by Robert MacDonald Publishing
Designed by Tony de Saulles

ISBN 0 00 219858 4

Typeset by Peter MacDonald Typesetting, London
Printed and bound in Great Britain by
William Collins Sons & Co Ltd, Glasgow.

Foreword

I have always been enthusiastic about wildlife, especially birds; but I've never been an out-and-out fanatic, as many of the characters in this book clearly are. This book celebrates the humorous and the outlandish in birdwatching — and I am delighted to see it. Bird-watching is a serious business, but it should never take itself so-lemnly. I am glad to see someone poking a little gentle fun at all of us.

Birdwatching *should* be fun. But of course it's not *only* fun. It's immensely enjoyable, but it's also immensely important. Without the large number of birdwatchers in Britain, and the information they collect, we would know far less about our birds. The future of our birds and wildlife depends on our knowing when they need to be protected and how best to go about it.

Although I have the honour to be President of the Royal Society for the Protection of Birds, I certainly cannot claim to know every-thing about birds — any more than I know all the answers to the questions I ask on Mastermind. This book is an opportunity to test your own knowledge, in either a serious or a light-hearted way. Anyone who can answer *all* the questions, (and no cheating, mind!) can fairly claim to be an ornithological 'mastermind' (or do I mean 'birdbrain'?).

Magnus Magnusson

Author's acknowledgements

Too many people to mention have contributed in some way to this book and my thanks go to all of them. Special thanks go to Neil Morris for helping to compile questions; Bill and Ruby at the 'Coot and Corncrake' for oiling the wheels; and all of the regulars who helped and encouraged me. I would also like to thank Ted and Jackie, who provided a quiet environment when needed, and to Penny who helped on the word processor. Thanks to Crispin Fisher who once again drew the delightful notebooks and the pub sign as well as contributing to the quizzes; Norman Arlott, whose magnificent owl graces the cover and Philip Snow who provided the hilarious cartoons. And I would particularly like to thank Robert MacDonald for his help with stories and for his eternal patience and hospitality.

Contents

Preface

To anyone who has read *Evenings at the Coot and Corncrake*, the contents of this book will come as no surprise. To a newcomer the existence of any such pub may appear spurious. There are, however, many pubs similar to the *Coot and Corncrake* and I am sure that all of them have their stories to tell.

I stumbled across the *Coot and Corncrake* many years ago and have become an infrequent but regular visitor there. Many happy evenings have been spent there in the company of other birders and I have heard many weird and wonderful tales. I have attempted to remember them as best I can although some details have become clouded with the passing of time (as the evenings wore on.)

Rossie, the landlord, has kindly let me use some of the quizzes which brighten up the dull winter evenings in the pub. Each quiz can be 'dipped into' or can be used as a more formal quiz with two teams of four players. Each quiz is composed of 64 questions, with the specific intention of being divided into eight rounds with four questions to each team per round. Two or more rounds could be treated as individual questions with the rest for the whole team.

Since the appearance of 'Evenings', many people have asked me if the pub exists and where it is. I always reply that, as I found it by chance, so should they, for its discovery gives just as much excitement as finding a new bird for Britain. Some readers may be familiar with it and may be worried that they will feature in these stories but I can assure them that every attempt has been made to preserve their anonymity and dignity.

I hope that everyone who reads this book will find something to both amuse and tax them and that anyone not familiar with birding will realise what a serious pastime it is.

Chris Harbard

Twitchett's Revenge

The *Coot and Corncrake* is a typical country pub which, for many years, has been the traditional watering hole for birdwatchers, who come from far and wide to visit the birdwatching sites locally. Anyone entering the pub unawares at the weekend will find it full of binoculars and beards, telescopes and tripods, wellingtons and waterproofs and the conversation, if overheard, can be perplexing to the uninitiated.

On most occasions, one voice dominates all and the booming words 'That reminds me...' mean that Twitchett is holding court. A more-or-less permanent resident of the pub, Twitchett is notorious for his birdwatching tales, particularly those concerning his ancestors who, in one way or another, have left a permanent mark or blemish on the birdwatching world.

He is a large man who bears the ruddy complexion that is due either to unaccustomed exposure to the sun or to overfamiliarity with alcohol. It soon becomes obvious which of these is applicable. Accompanying Twitchett will usually be his stalwart followers, Listman, Stickler and Stringwell. Behind the bar, the long-suffering landlord Rossie (who has always been known by this nickname, as he has never dared to let his birding clientele know that his name is Albert Ross) serves all with the patience that comes with years of dealing with what is clearly a bunch of lunatics. At the corner of the bar sits the Colonel, drinking gin and tonics and contemplating the Oval, or any other cricket ground he can remember, blissfully unaware of the real world around him.

'Phone for you Twitchett' shouted Rossie across the crowded bar.

'Good grief' said Twitchett, jumping to his feet, 'that's the first call I've had in weeks.' He manoeuvered his way to the bar and, as he picked up the phone, Listman and Stringwell listened eagerly, trying to catch a few words. Any call for Twitchell in the pub meant bird news and early October was a prime time for rarities. There was a time when, every Friday night, the 'phone in the *Coot and Corncrake* would ring continuously. Birders from every corner of the country would ring to find out the latest news and occasionally to pass on news of some fresh rarity. Recently the number of calls had fallen and now a call for Twitchett was itself a rarity. The reason for this sudden lack of communication was the formation of a birder's hot-line. Some enterprising young birders had set up a multi-line answerphone system which allowed instant access to regularly updated news about what birds were seen where each day.

Twitchett, naturally, was dead against it. 'It will never catch on.' he said when he first heard about it. 'These machines always break down and they're too damned impersonal. You'll never catch me ringing it. Never!'

Stringwell and Listman, however, thought it was rather a good idea and every day they rang the hot-line number, although they didn't always tell Twitchett this. Twitchett would complain bitterly that it had ruined his Friday evenings and most people suspected it was simply that he felt annoyed at not being the centre of attention when the phone rang.

The new system had given birders an extra degree of freedom. There was now no need to stay in on a Friday night in case of news. All you had to do was to keep in touch with the hot-line and, if there was news of a 'crippler', then you headed for home to arrange lifts. It was also available to anyone who subscribed and rumours had it that several thousand now did.

'What?' shouted Twitchett excitedly down the phone, his voice cutting across the hubbub of the bar. This was quickly followed by an equally loud 'Where?' and 'When was it seen?'. His voice suddenly lowered and the two eavesdroppers could see him nodding and writing something down in his notebook. They thought they could make out the words 'No one, not even ...' and 'But I couldn't do...' and finally 'Yes, straight away.'

Twitchett put the 'phone down and walked slowly back to the table, which had moved about six feet nearer the bar due to the inquisitive leaning of Stringwell and Listman.

'What is it?' the two of them chorused.

'Oh, nothing really.' said Twitchett. 'Just news of a... a Broadbilled at Breydon.'

'But I told you about that earlier.' said Listman.

'And Radde's at Radipole' he offered. 'Spoonbill at Spurn, Bluethroat at Blakeney... nothing to get excited about.'

'The way you shouted, I thought it must be at least a tattler at Titchwell' said Listman.

There was a loud crack as Twitchett bit through the stem of his pipe. The bowl and what remained of the stem, released from their usual fixed position, sailed upwards and disappeared down the cleavage of a well-built lady at the table next to them. She leapt up, knocking over the table which held two nearly full pints of lager, a gin and tonic and a strange concoction made from vodka, tonic, lime and blackcurrant. During the ensuing chaos Twitchett downed his beer with uncharacteristic speed, said 'Must dash, I'm supposed to be meeting someone', and then turned and left.

Listman and Stringwell stared at one another. 'Something fishy there.' said Listman. 'I'd stake my last five ticks that it was bird news – I've never seen Twitchett get excited about anything else.' At the next table, one of the pint of lager drinkers was trying to hit the other, thinking he had assaulted his girlfriend.

'He's definitely up to something.' agreed Stringwell as the strange concoction tried to pick her boyfriend up from the floor. 'But if it was news of a crippler he'd have told us, unless…'

'Never.'said Listman, shaking his head. 'Twitchett has always been against suppression and he wouldn't keep anything from us.' The gin and tonic recovered the remains of the pipe and tried to show it to her escort, who was hiding from a hail of blows from the strange concoction's handbag. 'The best thing to do is to ring the hot-line and see if there is any news on it.'

Twitchett was in quite a panic when he left the pub. The 'phone call had been from his old friend Grenville Hopper, who lived on the Sussex coast. Grenville, who was known to his birding friends as 'Gropper', usually spent his time birdwatching at Beachy Head, Chichester and Pagham Harbours, and Selsey Bill, and he'd found some good birds there in the past. Today, it sounded as though he'd found the big one but he needed someone else to confirm it, and so he had rung Twitchett.

The reason for his rather secretive call was that the bird was only visible from private land, so private that no-one was allowed near it, and he had been trespassing when he found it. He had chosen to ring Twitchett because he knew he was trustworthy and would understand his predicament, and also because he had visited the States and had knowledge of the identification problems involved. Listman's comment had been uncomfortably close to the truth, because the bird he had found was either a Grey-rumped Sandpiper or a Wandering Tattler.

Twitchett arrived at his friend's house just before dawn as had been arranged. Gropper explained that the land on which the bird had appeared was owned by a local farmer called Bush who allowed no access to it. The two of them set out under the cover of darkness, to reach the place where the bird had been seen at first light, and to cut down the chances of their being caught trespassing. The small creek where he had found the bird was about a mile away from the nearest road and, in the darkness, the walk was quite a challenge. There were three fences, two ditches and a small stream to negotiate and Twitchett began to wonder whether a run round Aintree might not have been easier.

Eventually they arrived at the muddy edge of the creek and crouched down. Gropper explained that high tide would be in about two hours time and that this would provide the best chance of seeing the bird. They waited. That waders were present had been obvious from their calls and, as dawn came, the birds slowly became visible. The wind was blowing coldly from the north and, as he crouched there shivering, Twitchett cursed the fact that he had forgotten to bring his usual hipflask of Glenmorangie.

'Not long now' said Gropper. 'It was with Redshank when I first saw it but they kept driving it off. It spent most of its time feeding on the far bank and at first I thought it was a strange looking Knot. It kept bobbing its tail and once it even perched on a small branch.'

'Did you hear it call?' asked Twitchett. 'The call is the best way to distinguish between the two tattlers, unless you get an extremely good look at them.'

'Not that I know of' said Gropper, 'but there were lots of waders calling, particularly Redshank, a few Curlew and Ringed Plover, and a Grey Plover which I didn't see. I also thought I heard a Jack Snipe but it was typically invisible.'

Their conversation was cut short by a rustling sound coming from the undergrowth behind them. Suddenly a huge black shape jumped out and began barking.

'My God, it's the gamekeeper's dog.' said Gropper. 'If he catches us here we're done for. We'll be lucky to get away with only buckshot in our backsides.'

Twitchett, who had been crouched for the last hour and a half, tried to stand up prior to fleeing. Unfortunately, both his legs had gone to sleep and instead of standing up he fell forward, down the edge of the creek, into the most evil-smelling mud he had ever come face to face with.

'B.....' he shouted, his profanity being cut short by a mouthful of mud. Gropper was in no position to help as the black beast had firmly clamped its jaws around his left leg – which had, at least for the moment, stopped it barking.

Twitchett struggled to the top of the bank. He was covered from head to toe in a sticky grey-brown slime which slowly oozed downwards under the force of gravity.

'Grr...' he spluttered, trying to call his friend. To the black beast, this strange apparition came as a complete surprise. As a young puppy it had suffered from innumerable nightmares because of its master's liking for horror films. Seeing what was clearly the result of crossing 'The Creature from the Black Lagoon' with 'The Blob' walking towards it growling, the unfortunate beast totally lost its sense of duty. With a yelp of fear, it released Gropper's leg, and ran off into the distance with its tail well and truly between its legs.

'Run for it' yelled Gropper. 'If the dog's here the gamekeeper can't be far behind.' As if in response, a loud shout came from the left of them. Twitchett started running, his vision still not completely free from mud. Gropper ran into a nearby copse and some birds crashed out of it with wings clapping.

Twitchett followed but the sound of a shotgun going off behind the trees caused him to change direction towards a line of poplars. He paused for breath behind one of them and then headed in what he thought was the direction of the road. After about a quarter of an hour he realised he was lost. On his way to the creek he had simply followed Gropper and now the fences, ditches and hedges all looked alike.

Eventually, he reached a road and followed it to where he thought Gropper had parked, but there was no sign of the car. Hoping that Gropper would return, he sat down and waited, until he was woken abruptly by the sound of an engine. A quick glance at his watch told him that two hours had passed. A police car came towards him, pulled up alongside and the driver wound down his window.

'Good morning' he said, eyeing Twitchett with some amusement. 'Been for a paddle have we?'

'Slipped in some mud' replied Twitchett, who couldn't help but notice that the number on the constable's shoulder was 424, exactly the number of birds on his British list.

'Really?' said the PC. 'You wouldn't have been on yonder land, would you?' He indicated the fields which Twitchett had crossed earlier. 'We had a report from a gamekeeper about people on his land. He said they did something to his best mastiff.'

'I don't know anything about it' said Twitchett, hoping that the gamekeeper hadn't seen him.

'Funny that, he found signs that someone had fallen in the creek there, and here you are covered in mud. I think perhaps you should come to the station with me, don't you?' The policeman opened the rear door of the car and Twitchett got in.

Twitchett sat in the car, thinking of the quiet day he had intended to spend and of how Gropper's call had changed everything. He had originally felt guilty at deceiving Listman and Stringwell, but now he was glad they were not with him. He hadn't caused any damage when he trespassed and anyway the police couldn't prove it was him. With a little embroidery this would make a marvellous tale in the pub. He sat back in the seat with a smile and reached into his top pocket for his pipe.

'The gamekeeper also found a pipe there' said the policeman. 'You wouldn't happen to smoke would you?'

'Gave it up' replied Twitchett, desperately trying not to cough, his tobacco pouch suddenly feeling like lead in his pocket.

They reached the police station and Twitchett was shown to a room marked 'Inspector' on the door. The room contained a desk, a number of chairs, a couple of filing cabinets and a painting of an albatross on the wall. Behind the desk sat a dark-haired man who looked up with piercing blue eyes as Twitchett entered.

'Mr Twitchett, I presume.' he said.

Twitchett's mind whirled. How did they know his name? A mist floated before his eyes and he began to feel dizzy.

'Get him a seat and then leave us' the Inspector ordered the constable. Twitchett sat shaking in the chair as the Inspector picked up what looked suspiciously like his birding notebook.

'Interesting reading this' he said with a half smile on his face. 'Nice sketches too, but I'm not sure that you correctly identified the female Pied Wheatear you saw, especially as you went mainly on the tail'.

At this Twitchett almost fell off his chair. He coughed, spluttered and began going red until the Inspector handed him his pipe and said 'Have a smoke, you'll feel better.'

Twitchett clutched for his pipe and filled it with shaking hands. As he lit it and sat back the Inspector leaned forward looking Twitchett straight in the eye. 'So where was this supposed tattler?' he asked. 'On Bush's land was it?'

Twitchett nodded. 'Did you see it?' asked the Inspector.

'No' said Twitchett forlornly.

'What a shame' said the Inspector 'it's new for the Western Palearctic I believe.' The Inspector told Twitchett the whole story. Unbeknown to Twitchett the tattler, which was in fact a Grey-rumped Sandpiper, had been located the previous day at a high tide wader roost near Pagham Harbour just before dusk. Final confirmation of the bird's identity hadn't been made until high tide that morning, when the news had been put out on the birder's hot-line. The local police had been informed about possible parking difficulties and so the Inspector knew all about the bird. He was, in fact, a keen birdwatcher himself and was hoping to get away later to see the bird.

'Now I know why you happen to have a picture of an albatross on your wall.' said Twitchett.

'Actually it reminds me of my wife.' replied the Inspector.

Twitchett now explained how he came to be in Bush's fields and, as he told the story, he began to feel as though he were already back in the *Coot and Corncrake*. The Inspector let him off with a caution and got a car to drive him to Gropper's house.

'I waited some time for you' explained Gropper. 'When you didn't arrive back at the car, I assumed the keeper had got you and drove home.' He had by now heard about the roost site of the tattler and was intending to visit it at the next high tide. 'Unfortunately it will be dark before tonight's high tide so tomorrow morning will be the first opportunity. You still mustn't give away its feeding area though.' he insisted to Twitchett. Twitchett agreed and then slowly a smile came over his face.

'Have you got a local 'phone book?' he asked. Gropper fetched it and gave it to him. Twitchett flicked through a few pages, made a note of a number and gave it back. 'Do you mind if I make a couple of calls? People will be wondering where I am.'

'Help yourself' said Gropper. 'Its in the hall.'

Twitchett stayed for lunch and then excused himself and drove home. In the evening he was in the bar at his usual table dead on nine o'clock. Stringwell and Listman came in soon afterwards and for the next hour Twitchett told them the story.

'Oh, one more thing' he said. 'Have you got the number for the hot-line, I'd like to give it a ring.'

Listman and Stringwell both choked on their beer and were coughing so much they had to write it down for him.

Twitchett went to the bar and dialled the number. He stood for a few minutes and then began to laugh. The whole bar went quiet as his bellowing drowned out any possible conversation. 'Come here and listen to this' he gasped to Listman and Stringwell.

They took the receiver and each listened.

'...Grey-rumped Sandpiper was seen at its roost at first light but not later in the afternoon. It has however been seen on private land nearby during the day and anyone wanting permission to look for it should ring Mr Bush on...'

'Maybe the 'phone isn't ringing here' said Twitchett, 'but I have a pretty good idea of where it *will* be ringing.'

Questions: *1*. What were the birds which Gropper flushed from the copse? *2*. What was the Inspector suggesting that the Pied Wheatear in Twitchett's notebook might be? *3*. What was Gropper's unlikely claim?

General Knowledge

Q1. What birds often help their parents raise a second brood?

Q2. What birds will help another pair to raise young if their own have failed?

Q3. What birds feed their young on 'milk'?

Q4. How many insects can a Swift carry in its gape? 100, 500, 1,500

Q5. How long does a Swift normally take to lay three eggs?

Q6. Which flies faster at cruising speed? Carrion Crow, Blue Tit or Swift?

Q7. How many species of waders breed regularly in Britain and Ireland?

Q8. How many species of warblers breed regularly in Britain and Ireland?

Q9. What is *Passer domesticus*?

Q10. What is *Sturnus vulgaris*?

Q11. How many members of the true tit family breed in Britain?

Q12. How many members of the true tit family breed in Ireland?

Q13. What two British birds are named after their piscivorous diet?

Q14. What two British birds are named after the berries they feed on?

Q15. The Egyptian god Thoth had the head of what bird?

Q16. The Egyptian god Horus had the head of what bird?

Q17. What type of bird was Huitzilopochtli, worshipped by the Aztecs?

Q18. Why do large numbers of Shelduck fly to the Friesian Islands?

Q19. What British breeding finch winters on the coast?

Q20. If you see a large pale Wheatear in spring, where is it flying to?

Q21. What is an egg tooth?

Q22. What does it mean if an egg is 'pipped'?

Q23. What wader has the most cosmopolitan distribution?

Q24. What bird is stuffed and displayed at Lords, having been killed there by a cricket ball?

Q25. The male of which British bird incubates the first clutch of eggs while the female lays and incubates a second?

Q26. What body officially admits birds onto the British and Irish list?

Q27. What is the family of birds whose members carry their young on their backs?

Q28. What bird carries its young between its legs as it flies?

Q29. What small bird habitually sings in flight?

Q30. How do you tell a juvenile from an adult Collared Dove?

Q31. What is *Cygnus cygnus*?

Q32. What is *Puffinus puffinus*?

Q33. What is a 'peep'?

Q34. What is subsong?

Q35. What is psittacism?

Q36. What was a garefowl?

Q37. How many species of ducks breed regularly in Britain and Ireland?

Q38. How many species of finches breed regularly in Britain and Ireland?

Q39. What is *Cuculus canorus*?

Q40. What is *Upupa epops*?

Q41. What British bird are mynah birds related to?

Q42. What British birds was the Dodo related to?

Q43. What was first seen in Lincolnshire in 1952 and first bred in Norfolk in 1955?

Q44. What bird is named after the way it can twist its head around?

Q45. Which of the three common woodpeckers doesn't drum?

Q46. When is a Black Guillemot not a black guillemot?

Q47. Why is the waxwing so-called?

Q48. What is *Branta canadensis*?

Q49. What is *Branta bernicla*?

Q50. What is unusual about the feet of grebes?

Q51. Which two British birds display in 'leks'?

Q52. Which is the smallest British goose?

Q53. Which is the largest British goose?

Q54. How can you identify individual Bewick's Swans?

Q55. What is the main prey of the Buzzard?

Q56. Why is a petrel so named?

Q57. What bird of prey has more than 50 per cent of its European population breeding in Britain?

Q58. Place the following plovers in order of size: Little Ringed, Ringed and Kentish.

Q59. Where are the breeding areas of the two races of Black-tailed Godwit that occur in Britain?

Q60. Why is a Redpoll so named?

Q61. Why is a Dunnock so named?

Q62. What is *Rallus aquaticus*?

Q63. What is *Phasianus colchicus*?

Q64. What is the difference between adult and immature Mistle thrushes?

Sketchbook

california condors . P.S.

P.S.

While visiting friends in Wales,
Twitchett decided to spend European
Bird Day at an R.S.P.B. reserve nearby.
These are some of the notes he took.

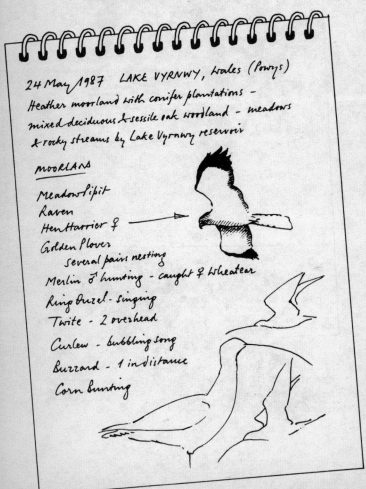

24 May 1987   LAKE VYRNWY, Wales (Powys)
Heather moorland with conifer plantations –
mixed deciduous & sessile oak woodland – meadows
& rocky streams by Lake Vyrnwy reservoir

MOORLAND

Meadow Pipit
Raven
Hen Harrier ♀
Golden Plover
        several pairs nesting
Merlin ♂ hunting – caught ♀ Wheatear
Ring Ouzel – singing
Twite – 2 overhead
Curlew – bubbling song
Buzzard – 1 in distance
Corn Bunting

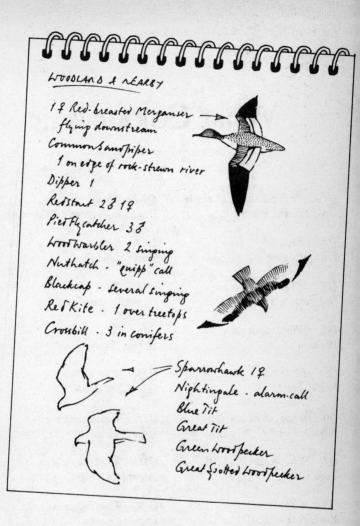

WOODLAND & NEARBY

1 ♀ Red-breasted Merganser —→
   flying downstream
Common Sandpiper
   1 on edge of rock-strewn river
Dipper 1
Redstart 2 ♂ 1 ♀
Pied Flycatcher 3 ♂
Wood Warbler 2 singing
Nuthatch - "quipp" call
Blackcap - several singing
Red Kite - 1 over treetops
Crossbill - 3 in conifers

Sparrowhawk 1 ♀
Nightingale - alarm-call
Blue Tit
Great Tit
Green Woodpecker
Great Spotted Woodpecker

Question: Twitchett was plainly not
having a good day. There are six
mistakes in these notes. What are they?

25

What Colour is...?

Q1. What colour are a Canada Goose's legs?

Q2. What colour are a Shelduck's legs?

Q3. What colour are an Oystercatcher's legs?

Q4. What colour are a Pochard's eyes?

Q5. What colour is a Ruddy Duck's bill?

Q6. What colour is a Moorhen's bill?

Q7. What colour is a Little Tern's bill?

Q8. What colour is a Kingfisher's throat?

Q9. What colour is a Redstart's back?

Q10. What colour is a Stonechat's rump?

Q11. What colour is a male Bearded Tit's head?

Q12. What colour are a Brambling's outer tail feathers?

Q13. What colour are a Starling's legs?

Q14. What colour is a Gadwall's speculum?

Q15. What colour is a Reed Bunting's rump?

Q16. What colour is a Goosander's back?

Q17. What colour are a Kestrel's legs?

Q18. What colour are a Moorhen's wings?

Q19. What colour is a Lapwing's neck?

Q20. What colour is a Spotted Redshank's spots?

Q21. What colour are a Grey Phalarope's cheeks?

Q22. What colour is a Wood Pigeon's tail?

26

Q23. What colour is a Mistle Thrush's underwing?

Q24. What colour is a Song Thrush's underwing?

Q25. What colour is a Magpie's rump?

Q26. What colour is a House Sparrow's rump?

Q27. What colour are a Blackcap's outer tail feathers?

Q28. What colour is a Turnstone's rump?

Q29. What colour are a Kentish Plover's legs?

Q30. What colour is a Sabine's Gull's bill?

Q31. What colour are a Water Rail's legs?

Q32. What colour are a Mallard's legs?

Q33. What colour is a Gannet's bill?

Q34. What colour is a Herring Gull's eye-ring?

Q35. What colour is a Lesser Black-backed Gull's eye-ring?

Q36. What colour is a Grey Wagtail's rump?

Q37. What colour is a Pied Wagtail's rump?

Q38. What colour is a Bee-eater's throat?

Q39. What colour is a Golden Oriole's rump?

Q40. What colour is a Treecreeper's rump?

Q41. What colour is a Wood Warbler's belly?

Q42. What colour is a Lesser Spotted Woodpecker's rump?

Q43. What colour are a Sandwich Tern's legs?

Q44. What colour are a Grey Wagtail's legs?

Q45. What colour are a Yellow Wagtail's legs?

Q46. What colour are a Water Pipit's outer tail feathers?

Q47. What colour is a Cirl Bunting's throat?

Q48. What colour are a Long-eared Owl's eyes?

Q49. What colour are a Short-eared Owl's eyes?

Q50. What colour is a Ptarmigan's breast in summer?

Q51. What colour is a Long-tailed Duck's throat?

Q52. What colour are a Blackbird's legs?

Q53. What colour are a Mistle Thrush's legs?

Q54. What colour are a Blue Tit's legs?

Q55. What colour is a Snow Bunting's back?

Q56. What colour are a Lapwing's legs?

Q57. What colour are a Dotterel's legs?

Q58. What colour is a Wood Pigeon's bill?

Q59. What colour is a Turtle Dove's bill?

Q60. What colour is a Redpoll's bill?

Q61. What colour is a Linnet's bill?

Q62. What colour is a Marsh Harrier's tail?

Q63. What colour are a Grey Partridge's legs?

Q64. What colour are a Mute Swan's legs?

The Ju-ju

It was a summer evening at the *Coot and Corncrake*. Outside, the rain poured steadily down and a cold north-easterly rattled the window panes. Inside, a small group of regulars was remonstrating with the landlord.

'It's perishing in here' complained Listman, his already sallow features taking on a distinct bluish tinge. 'Like a morgue' agreed Twitchett. 'Come on Rossie, light the fire. You can't expect us to sit and drink in this temperature; we're not eskimoes.' An icicle seemed to be forming on the end of Stringwell's nose.

Rossie didn't seem anxious to oblige. 'It's the middle of June' he grumbled. 'The wood's out in the woodshed, and anyway' he added, following a train of thought that was obscure to everyone else 'I've just fed the chickens.' Two or three drops of water rolled off his hair and fell on to the bar.

'In that case,' said Listman sternly, 'we shall be forced to ask Twitchett to tell us about the time he was marooned on an iceberg while in pursuit of a Labrador Duck. Again.'

Within ten minutes the fire was blazing merrily and Twitchett, Stringwell, Stickler and Listman were seated in their accustomed places, tankards newly refilled. Listman had produced a large, garishly coloured brochure from his pocket and was studying it with close attention. 'What on earth is that?' demanded Twitchett, stretching out a hand. Listman held the brochure up for all to see:

'FLY-BY-NIGHT TOURS', it said in large purple letters; 'a bird watcher's dream come true.' *'Fantastic specialty tours for birdwatchers'* it continued, as though afraid that it might not have made its point, 'the birdwatcher's holiday of a lifetime, special reduced rates available NOW!!!'

The company observed this work of art in stunned silence. Beneath the lettering, the brochure sported a picture of a dark-skinned girl in a very brief bikini playing with a beach ball, while what looked like a stuffed parrot surveyed her from the branch of a palm tree.

'You're not serious, of course' remarked Twitchett.

'Well... er...'. Listman seemed rather sheepish. 'It's just that with this horrible weather, and since I've got a couple of weeks holiday coming to me, I did think... Well, it's time I did something for my life list. And anyway, it's jolly cheap' he ended lamely.

Twitchett had meanwhile seized the brochure and was turning through the pages. 'What had you in mind?' he asked, chortling. 'Thinking of New Guinea were you – "Join our hand-picked experts on an epic voyage of exploration through the valley of the head-hunters to the remote fastnesses that are the home of the legendary bower birds. Be amazed at their shimmering arabesques; be stunned by... ".'

Listman interrupted this recitation, and snatched back the brochure from Twitchett's hand. 'I don't know what you find so funny. Just because you've never been further than the South of France... '

'Not true... ' Twitchett started to protest. But Listman, by now quivering with indignation, was not to be stopped. 'I have decided that I shall go to equatorial Africa. And you lot can be as jealous as you like.'

Stringwell was shaking his head in mock sorrow, and Twitchett was rumbling with mirth. 'Off to the Cacobambo Valley, are you?', he said, 'to look for the winter home of the Waldrapp?'. And he started to laugh so much that he nearly fell off his chair.

Listman went very red. 'I don't see why I shouldn't' he said, after Twitchett had subsided. 'At least the sun will be shining.'

Twitchett suddenly stopped laughing and looked at Listman with disbelief. 'You're not serious' he said. 'Don't you know about the place?'

'Only what it says in here' said Listman, reading from the brochure; '...an adventure beyond compare; a true apotheosis for..'

'What's a potheosis?' interrupted Stringwell, 'do they mean a polyonymus? And isn't that... '

'No, no, no,' boomed Twitchett; 'haven't you ever heard of the "Birdwatcher's Grave"?'

'The birdwatcher's grave?' echoed Stringwell, Stickler and Listman, staring wide-eyed at Twitchett.

'No, I see you haven't' said Twitchett. 'Well, I can tell you that the Cacobambo valley has a thoroughly unsavoury reputation, and one that is richly deserved. No white man has set foot in the valley since the turn of the century, and of several Victorian birdwatchers known to have visited the place, only one ever came out alive: a woman.'

'A woman?' chanted Stringwell and Listman, who seemed to have lost the power of independent speech.

'A woman!' repeated Twitchett, as he settled back in his chair and started to refill his pipe. 'Obviously,' he said, a contented smile beginning to spread over his face, 'I've never told you the story of my great-great aunt Floralinda.'

'My great-great aunt Floralinda was the daughter of my great-great-great grandfather Jeremiah Twitchett, who made a fortune early in the industrial revolution by manufacturing cast-iron treadmills. Floralinda's mother had died in childbirth, and she and her fourteen brothers and sisters were sternly and strictly brought up by their father and a succession of housekeepers and tutors. Unfortunately, because of an early indiscretion – she returned a smile bestowed on her by one of the demonstrators of her father's treadmills – Floralinda was allowed no suitors. While her brothers and sisters married and moved away, she devoted her youth entirely to good works and to penitential sessions on the treadmill installed in the parlour at home.

'It was in the course of the first of these pursuits that she made the acquaintance of the local vicar, who happened to be none other than that great Victorian naturalist and pioneer ornithologist, Wyckliffe Bagginshaw. It was he who first enthused her with a love of birds, and the two spent many hours – in the course of doing good works – recording and discussing their observations of the countryside around. Floralinda is, in fact credited as "my sweet muse" in Bagginshaw's immortal *Ave, O Ave Aves, Some reflections on the divinity of our Feathered Friends*, and Floralinda's watercolour "Ruffled feathers; a Nightingale in a storm", which was shown at the Royal Academy in 1858, was dedicated to him in return.

'When Jeremiah died suddenly of apoplexy – apparently, somebody had predicted that Disraeli would become leader of the Tory party – Floralinda was left with a substantial fortune, some very large muscles acquired on the domestic treadmill, a deep love of birds and a suddenly awakened appetite for adventure. After discussion with the Rev. Bagginshaw, she decided that she would set out to resolve one of the great mysteries of Victorian ornithology, the whereabouts of the winter home of the Waldrapp which, if you remember, was then thought to be somewhere in equatorial Africa.

'It's a great pity', said Twitchett, pausing to empty his pint, 'that Floralinda's own account of her travels no longer survives. Thank you another pint of best please. She did of course write copious letters to the Rev. Bagginshaw and even the small proportion that survived the native postal services occupied three cabin trunks. Her personal journals, I was told, ran to twenty-eight volumes. All, alas, have now gone. My great uncle 'Tally-ho' Twitchett (the great horseman), who told me what I know about Floralinda, heard the story himself from his great-grandfather Eustace; and Eustace had actually seen many of the papers. When I tried to discover their whereabouts now, I was told that the whole lot had been burned by Canon (he had been promoted) Bagginshaw's sister. Tragic!

'Anyway, the outlines of the story are clear. Floralinda set out from Liverpool in 1863 or '64 on board a slaver bound for the Congo. She whiled away the several weeks on board by sketching her observations of Gannets, Brown Boobies, Red-tailed Tropic-birds and magnificent Frigate-birds, and by writing eulogies of mother nature in her diaries. On arrival in Africa, she set about organising her trip to the hinterland with characteristic Victorian insensitivity and vigour. Since no lady of consequence travelled lightly in Victorian times, she had come well equipped for more or less any eventuality. Her baggage train consisted of 140 bearers, no less than six of whom were required to carry just the cast-iron steam-driven fly swat that Jeremiah had tried so hard to patent while he was alive.

'She was not helped in her journey by having only the slightest idea of where she wanted to go, and nothing but an old school atlas on which to indicate her destination. The atlas, of course meant nothing to the bearers; they had never seen one before and Africa to them must have looked like the back end of an elephant. Neverthe-less, Floralinda was fully endowed with the Twitchett character-istics of courage, determination and fortitude and eventually she persuaded her retinue to set out.

'The bearers, of course, spoke no English. They belonged to one of the tribes whose contact with British slavers had given them a sort of smattering of English words, but to which they had attached their own private meanings. The language was called gobspik, and it evidently contained no word for "bird", and certainly nothing for "Waldrapp".

'Floralinda recorded at great length in her journals her attempts to make her porters understand – she had to reenact whole scenes of bird behaviour, flying, preening and all the rest of it – before they appeared to grasp her meaning. It was the preening that did it apparently; after her enactment of a preening ritual, they seemed to get the point and thereafter greeted the words 'bird' or 'Waldrapp' with shouts of laughter and exaggerated caricatures of avian preen-ing behaviour. And at the same time, they constantly reiterated the words 'cacobambo, cacobambo', pointing in unison towards the west. In fact, during the many months of weary travel through increasingly impenetrable jungle, this became almost a regular evening ritual. As my aunt retired to her toilette behind the care-fully erected chintz walls, the cries would go up around the camp fire 'Waldrapp, Waldrapp' and 'cacobambo, cacobambo', and there would be much hilarity, preening and leaping around.

'It is at this stage, according to my great uncle 'Tally-ho', who got it from his great-grandfather Eustace, that Floralinda's journals took on a slightly different tone. There is less and less about the glories of nature, and rather more about the native bearers. She was on record as wondering whether birds might not after all have been better off if the Creator had endowed them with smooth, dark, supple skins rather than feathers, and with finely sculptured, lissom limbs rather than with wings. And although she always concluded that Creator must have got it right, one could sense doubts. Floralinda had, of course, been deprived of male company throughout her life (with the exception of Rev., later Canon, Bagginshaw) and one can only imagine what effect the close proximity of 140 young native porters might have had on such a refined sensibility. Or perhaps' Twitchett seemed to reflect, 'it would be better not to.'

'There appears to have been no signs of Waldrapps throughout this time. Floralinda reports quite a few wintering European birds – Yellow Wagtails, Spotted Flycatchers, Willow Warblers and even (though I think this must be doubtful) an Arctic Warbler. It is even possible that she made one of the earliest records of the Congo Peacock, since that is what her description of an unidentified type of guineafowl sounds like.

'After about five months of trekking through the jungle, the porters began to get mutinous. Apparently they had got into the habit of stopping at various pools and hot springs on the journey, and importuning my aunt with cries of 'Waldrapp, Waldrapp', rubbing themselves and each other with warm mud and gesturing towards the pool. On each occasion, it proved to be a false alarm. No Waldrapps appeared and my aunt would peremptorily order the procession to continue. It can only have been her Twitchett strength of character (with a bit of help from the steam-driven fly-swat, which turned out to be useful after all) that enabled her to retain control.

'Eventually, amid growing excitement from the native bearers, they arrived at a deep valley, at the centre of which was a large mist-shrouded clearing. 'Cacobambo', they kept repeating as they pointed into the valley below.

'Darkness had descended before they had completed their climb down the steep sides of the valley, so they made camp for the night on the edge of the clearing itself. And so it was that my aunt woke next morning to be greeted by an astonishing sight. There in front of her were half-a-dozen bubbling hot pools, each attended by a tall and striking native who appeared to be carrying something that looked suspiciously like a towel. But more important than this, according to a postscipt added some time later to her journal, was the sight of a Waldrapp, preening and bathing not ten feet from her eyes. "The sight of this dear bird, hardly further away than my own hand," she wrote "representing as it did the successful culmination of much toil and endeavour, afforded me such intense pleasure that I had barely time to bless the name of our Maker who hath wrought such marvels, before I passed into a swoon, from which I was not to recover for some time." '

'According to the British Consul at Wagapopo, the nearest port on the river to Cacobambo, my aunt was delivered to him, still in a trance, by a team of 140 bearers some three months after the last entry in her journal. They had apparently returned to the valley some days after leaving Floralinda and, noting her immobility, had decided to carry her to the nearest outpost of civilisation. They accepted several articles of jewellery and the cast-iron fly-swat in payment for their efforts, and departed with strange nods, winks and nudges, calling out 'Waldrapp, Waldrapp' and laughing loudly as they departed.

'My aunt recovered from her trance after a short stay in the mission hospital although, according to the consul's report, they could not eradicate the fixed look of ecstasy that must have crossed her face when she encountered the Waldrapp in the clearing. The consul and the missionaries tried to persuade her to return home to England by the first available boat, but to no avail. She was adamant that she had to return to Cacobambo to carry out further studies of the Waldrapp, and to confirm that she had indeed found its winter resting place. After putting her effects in order, she completed her journal and entrusted it to the Consul for onward transmission to the Rev. Bagginshaw, hired 134 native bearers and set off for Cacobambo once again. She was never seen again.'

Twitchett fell silent, as though silently mourning the passing of his great-great-great aunt. Stringwell was the first to respond.

'Poppycock.' He said. 'Drivel. Even if your aunt had stumbled across a Waldrapp, I doubt if she could have recognised it. And anyway, I don't believe for a moment that this aunt of yours ever existed.'

'Oddly enough, I do have one relic of my aunt Floralinda' announced Twitchett, stirring himself in his chair. 'It's this' he said.

Stringwell and Listman sat and watched disbelievingly while Twitchett, struggling slightly with his waistcoat, produced a bunch of keys. 'This', he told them, pointing to the small wooden object which held the key-ring, 'is a ju-ju. It was obviously carved by one of the bearers during the journey as a good luck charm to ensure a successful outcome to the quest. It bears a crude but unmistakeable resemblance to a Waldrapp. My aunt left several of these in the missionary hospital in Wagapopo, and they were duly forwarded to the next of kin by the Consul when they had given up hope of her return. I got mine from my father, who got it from his and so on.'

'Let's have a look at that' demanded Listman suddenly. He took the key-ring and studied the wooden object intently. 'I thought as much' he said. He reached out and picked up the brochure. 'Look at this' he commanded, opening the brochure up to display the glories of the equatorial African tour. He pointed to a picture of a small wooden carved object. 'What's that?'

Stickler began to giggle. So did Stringwell. All three of them were soon roaring with helpless laughter. 'Waldrapp, Waldrapp' they chorused, before collapsing into hysterics again.

Twitchett was getting increasingly irritated and made several ineffective attempts to grab the brochure from their hands. 'Just what are you all laughing about?' he thundered.

'Listen to this' said Listman, between sobs of laughter.' "Among the many other pleasures to be found at Cacobambo is the traditional one of Sauna and Massage, known in the local language 'gobspik' as 'Waaldrep'. Amid the free and easy natives, you will find everything to meet your tastes. And to make your stay even more enjoyable, we will even issue you with one of the traditional tokens for a free session in one of the numerous private hot pools." '

He held out the brochure for Twitchett to see. There, an unmistakable replica of aunt Floralinda's ju-ju, was a free sauna and massage token.

Questions: *1.* Why would Twitchett's story about his experience of being marooned on an iceberg be far-fetched? *2.* Which of Floralinda's observations from the boat was erroneous? *3.* Why was the Arctic Warbler she claimed doubtful?

What's the difference?

Q1. What is the difference between male and female Starlings in summer?

Q2. What is the difference between male and female Ruff in winter?

Q3. What is the difference between the leg colour of a Willow Warbler and a Chiffchaff?

Q4. What is the difference between the leg feathers of a Rook and a Carrion Crow?

Q5. What is the difference between the crowns of a Marsh Tit and a Willow Tit?

Q6. What is the difference between Pied Wagtails and White Wagtails?

Q7. What is the difference between an adult and a young Swallow in flight?

Q8. What is the difference between an adult and a young Goldcrest?

Q9. What is the difference between the incubation of House Martins and Swallows?

Q10. What is the difference between an Oystercatcher in summer and in winter?

Q11. What is the difference between the two European races of Bluethroat?

Q12. What is the difference between West European and Scandinavian Lesser Black-backed Gulls?

Q13. What is the difference between a British Dipper and a Continental one?

Q14. What is the difference between British and Northern European Long-tailed Tits?

Q15. What is the difference between male and female Mute Swans?

Q16. What is the difference between a male and a female Nightjar in flight?

Q17. What is the difference between nest sites of Long-eared Owls and Short-eared Owls?

Q18. What is the difference between nest sites of Spotted Flycatchers and Pied Flycatchers?

Q19. What is the difference between the main foods of Crossbill and Scottish Crossbill?

Q20. What is the difference between Greenland and Russian Brent Geese?

Q21. What is the difference between the underparts of adult and juvenile Peregrines?

Q22. What is the difference between the tails of a Whinchat and a Stonechat?

Q23. What is the difference between adult and young Ring-necked Parakeets?

Q24. What is the difference between adult and juvenile White-fronted Geese?

Q25. What is the difference between the display of Whitethroat and Lesser Whitethroat?

Q26. What is the difference between the moult of Red-throated Divers and Black-throated Divers?

Q27. What is the difference between the bills of Black-necked and Slavonian Grebes?

Q28. What is the difference between the bills of Red-necked and Great Crested Grebes?

Q29. What is the difference between the bills of buntings and warblers?

Q30. What is the difference between the bills of Whooper Swans and Bewick's Swans?

Q31. What is the difference between female Scaup and Tufted Duck?

Q32. What is the difference between the head colour of male Scaup and Tufted Ducks?

Q33. What is the difference between Common Scoter and Velvet Scoter in flight?

Q34. What is the difference between Ringed Plover and Little Ringed Plovers in flight?

Q35. What is the difference between a supercilium and an eye-stripe?

Q36. What is the difference between an orbital ring and an eye-ring?

Q37. What is the difference between the head patterns of adult Little Terns and adult Common Terns?

Q38. What is the difference between the head patterns of adult Little Gulls and adult Mediterranean Gulls?

Q39. What is the difference between the food of Bearded Tits in summer and in winter?

Q40. What is the difference between the food of Eiders and Cormorants?

Q41. What is the difference between the feeding methods of Mallard and Tufted Duck?

Q42. What is the difference between the feeding methods of Sparrowhawks and Kestrels?

Q43. What is the difference between the toes of Nuthatch and Great Spotted Woodpecker?

Q44. What is the difference between the toes of a Great Northern Diver and a Shag?

Q45. What is the difference between the tail patterns of juvenile and adult Kittiwake?

Q46. What is the difference between the tail patterns of Rock Dove and a Stock Dove?

Q47. What is the difference between the calls of Redshank and Greenshank?

Q48. What is the difference between the calls of Chaffinch and Brambling in winter.

Q49. What is the difference between the underwings of adult Little Gulls and adult Mediterranean Gulls?

Q50. What is the difference between the underwings of the two pratincoles that occur in Britain?

Q51. What is the difference between the tail shapes of Guillemots and Razorbills?

Q52. What is the difference between the tail shapes of Reed Warbler and Icterine Warbler?

Q53. What is the difference between the bill colour of male and female Bearded Tits?

Q54. What is the difference between the bill colour of male and female Goldeneye?

Q55. What is the difference between the food of Great Spotted Woodpecker and Green Woodpecker?

Q56. What is the difference between the food of Little Tern and Black Tern?

Q57. What is the difference between the bill shape of Bar-tailed Godwits and Black-tailed Godwits?

Q58. What is the difference between the bill colour of adult Little Ringed Plovers and adult Ringed Plovers?

Q59. What is the difference between the wing shapes of Sparrowhawks and Kestrels?

Q60. What is the difference between the wing colours of Carrion and Hooded Crows?

Q61. What is the difference between the sizes of male and female Capercaillies?

Q62. What is the difference between the sizes of male and female Sparrowhawks?

Q63. What is the difference between the nest sites of a Rock Pipit and a Tree Pipit?

Q64. What is the difference between the nest sites of a Reed Warbler and a Reed Bunting?

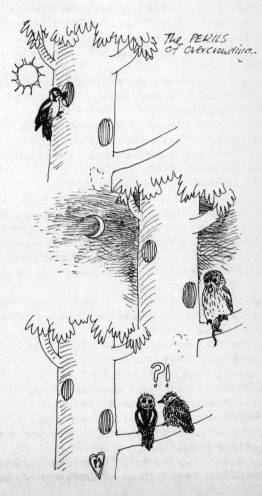

The PERILS of overcrowding..

The Collectors

The usually lively corner table in the *Coot and Corncrake* was, for once, rather subdued when Twitchett walked in. Stringwell looked positively morose, Listman was silent, and as for Stickler...

'My God, Stickler' boomed Twitchett 'you've not lost your hat, have you?'

'No' said Stickler, who was renowned for always looking as though he were about to mount an assault on the North Pole. 'I've removed it out of respect.'

Twitchett decided that a drink was in order before he enquired as to the the reasons for the funereal atmosphere.

'Pint of Best please Rossie, and a packet of those crunchy things that taste like barbecued swan droppings.'

'You don't have to choose those' said Rossie.

'Well the others taste like...'

'Not in front of the customers' said Rossie, looking around worriedly. 'I had enough trouble last time when you suggested that the bottle of Grouse was actually full of grouse... well, you remember'.

'But how was I to know that he was a Weights and Measures man, he didn't look like one, and anyway you passed the inspection he gave you with flying colours.'

'I agree' shouted the Colonel from his stool by the bar, 'don't believe a word they say. Different upbringing you know. Never make good umpires.'

Twitchett shook his head and wandered over to the corner where his usual chair was vacant, ready for him.

'So why all the long faces?' he asked.

'Didn't you see on the news about the poor old condor' said Listman. 'That's another one gone for good. I knew I should have gone to the States last year instead of trying for a big year list.'

'They've just captured the last one from the wild so now the twenty odd left are all in zoos', explained Stringwell.

'A great shame' said Twitchett. 'They were my great-grandfather Peregrine's favourite bird. He always made a point of going to see

40

them whenever he found himself in America, which was pretty often. His description of flocks of them soaring over the Grand Canyon...'

'Wait a minute' said Listman 'the Grand Canyon's in Arizona and the condor was confined to California.'

'But they're big birds – they cover a large territory' retorted Twitchett. He banged out his pipe very noisily and then realised it was empty anyway.

'What caused their demise?' asked Stickler.

'A combination of factors' answered Listman, 'destruction of the habitat, poisoning and I dare say egg-collectors took their toll...'

'Not in the States' interrupted Twitchett. 'Egg-collecting is a curiously British form of kleptomania. They should punish the blighters more severely.'

'I'd string them up' said Stickler.

'You usually do' said Listman. Stickler scowled as everyone laughed.

'Now that reminds me of a story about Lord Harringshaw' said Twitchett leaning back in his all too familiar way. 'I must have mentioned him – a good friend of my grandfather. He had an estate in Wales, near Snowdonia, I visited there when I was a lad, saw my first Golden Eagle there.' He paused to search for a pipe-cleaner.

'Anyway, I remember deciding to go back there for a hiking trip during one of the college holidays. One evening I had just made it to a village before dark and had been directed to the local pub for some lodgings. It was a strange place and the name itself should have warned me. It was called the *Drill and Blowpipe* and was a fairly small and dingy establishment. As so often happens when you are in a strange part of the country, all heads turned to watch me as I walked in, but on this occasion I felt they were being more than inquisitive.

'I asked the landlord if he had a room and noticed him glance across at a large man sitting in the corner who gave an almost imperceptible nod. He offered me a room in the back, just for one night, so I left my belongings there and wandered back to the bar for a pint or two. I had walked a lot that day and was relieved to be able to sit down with a drink and jot down some notes about the birds I had seen. I was particularly pleased with the number of spring migrants – Blackcap, Willow Warbler, Sedge Warbler, Marsh Warbler, Swallow, Sand Martin, Wheatear, and even a Ring Ousel, if I remember. However, I had hardly started writing when my attention was distracted by the people at the next table. They had a map spread out in front of them, which they were studying closely, and I wondered if they were hiking too. One of them was about my age and I assumed the other was probably his father. They were talking fairly quietly, but I couldn't help overhearing odd bits of conversation. I thought I heard one of them mention Merlin and, as I listened, various other words like "Raven", "Kite" and "displaying" drifted across. Naturally I thought they must be birdwatchers and so I leaned across and said "Have you seen any Peregrines around here?".

'The effect of my words was dramatic. The older man swept the map away and the whole pub went silent. In a flash the large man from the corner was beside me.

' "What do you want with Peregrines?" he asked sternly.

' "I used to visit round here when I was younger, and often saw them. I just wondered if they were still here" I said.

' "We don't talk about them to strangers" said the man. "You'd best mind your own business." With that he walked back to his corner.

'It was nearly closing time and I'd finished my beer so I decided it would be prudent to retire. Lying in my room, I pondered over the events of the evening. Why had the people in the pub reacted like that? Did they have something to hide? My thoughts were interrupted by the sound of footsteps and voices outside my window. Quietly I got out of bed and tiptoed to the open window. Peering out into the gloom, I could just about make out two figures whom I recogised as the two from the next table.

' "I'll meet you here tomorrow evening" said the older man. "I'll have all the gear. We'll head for the Devil's Crag at midnight." My heart skipped a beat at the words Devil's Crag. It was the name of a cliff face on Lord Harringshaw's estate where I had once watched Peregrines nesting. Suddenly it all became clear: the two were egg-collectors. The question now was what to do. The Lord Harringshaw my grandfather knew had died some years ago and had been succeeded by his son. I didn't know whether the new Lord Harringshaw was as avid a bird-watcher as his father, who had always vigorously guarded the Peregrines. All I could do was to pay him a visit the following day.'

'I'd have called the police' said Listman.

'It wouldn't have helped' explained Twitchett, 'because at that time the Protection of Birds Act hadn't been passed. My only possible source of help was Lord Harringshaw. He drained his glass, which was refilled by Stickler who was so engrossed in Twitchett's tale that he had not yet replaced his hat.

'The following morning I went straight to Lord Harringshaw's house. I introduced myself and was shown through to the library. Lord Harringshaw was a tall willowy figure, dressed in a long maroon dressing gown, which reminded me that the family had a curious habit of only getting dressed when they went out, and then not always. "You must be young Twitchett" he said, "sit down." He indicated a chair by the desk which was covered in paper and pots of paint. "Knew your grandfather well, sorry to hear he'd popped off."

'I agreed it was a shame and then went on to recount the tale of the previous evening. All the time I was telling it, Lord Harringshaw showed what appeared to be complete indifference. Apart from nodding his head a couple of times, he didn't say a word. When I had finished he simply thanked me for visiting, shook my hand, and summoned his butler to show me out.

' "But aren't you going to do anything about it?" I asked.

' "More pressing matters" he muttered and turned back to the volume he had been reading when I arrived.

'I walked off rather dazed and decided that, if he wouldn't help, then I would have to do something myself. That evening I hid along the road which passed by the Devil's Crag. It was a clear night and as I began walking towards the crag, which was about a mile away, I could hear Nightjars and Tawny Owls in the distance, and a Grasshopper Warbler was calling from a nearby bush. After about ten minutes I heard noises in front of me and so ducked behind a tree. Two figures approached, one helping the other along.

' "I think its broken" I heard the younger man say. "You didn't have the rope tight enough."

' "Never mind" said the other, "we're nearly back and we got the full clutch." As they drew level with the tree, I could see that the young man's arm was tied in a makeshift sling and he was limping. The other had some rope over his shoulder and a box under his arm. I stepped out from behind the tree. "I'll take those" I said, trying to sound brave and brandishing a large stick that I'd picked up. The older man swung round while his partner stumbled on. "You'll not get these, lad" he said and threw some rope at me. As I disentangled myself he ran off holding the box in his hands. I picked up the rope and was very thankful for a trick that my great-grandfather Peregrine had taught me as a youngster. With a quick twist I had a lasso and I ran after the man, carefully coiling the rope as I ran. As he reached the road I threw the rope and caught him around the neck. I saw him drop the box as I pulled on the rope.

The next thing I knew, I was coming round with my head feeling as though it would explode and with a lump even bigger than a Peregrine's egg on the back of it. I must have been hit by the fellow's accomplice and lain there for some time, as it was now nearly dawn. I struggled to my feet and walked to the road. Just as I reached it, I noticed something in the grass – an egg. They must have dropped one of them and been unable to find it.' Twitchett began to chuckle at this point. The chuckle grew into a laugh and tears began to trickle down his cheeks. 'I wonder if they know even now' he said.

'Know what?' asked his audience.

'Well I was feeling rather groggy after being hit and the nearest house belonged to Lord Harringshaw. I can remember walking there and banging on the door, and then I must have passed out. The next thing I know, I'm inside and being given some brandy. Lord Harringshaw was standing there. "They've taken them" I said. "I did warn you." I reached into my jacket and took out the egg. "You could have stopped them" I shouted.

' "Give me the egg and tell me what happened" he said, and when I'd finished he walked to the window which was beginning to be covered with spots of rain. "Come over here a moment." I struggled to my feet and walked over. "What do you see?" he asked, holding out his hand.

' "A cold Peregrine's egg" I replied.

' "Watch" he said , and proceeded to open the window and hold the egg out in the rain. "Now look" he said, bringing in his hand. Where the rain had fallen on the egg I could see the colour begin to lighten and run. I looked at him with my mouth open. "Chicken's egg" he said "painted it myself. I've got the real eggs stored in an incubator. That nest has got robbed every year now and I thought it was time to do something about it. Now how about breakfast. It'll have to be sausage and bacon, I used the last egg for..." '

Questions: *1*. Which migrant did Twitchett wrongly claim to have seen, and what was it more likely to have been? *2*. What other bird did he definitely misidentify? *3*. Which other bird is he unlikely to have seen, and what is he likely to have seen instead?

44

Dude's Quiz

Since a dude is one whose interest in birds remains at a normal level of sanity, these questions are generally easier than those in the other quizzes in the book. But beware; they are not without their pitfalls.

Q1. From which wild species is the London pigeon descended?

Q2. Which gull calls its own name?

Q3. Which bird 'booms'?

Q4. What is the difference between the male and female Song Thrush?

Q5. What bird is the pub named after in the song 'Pop goes the Weasel'?

Q6. What is the name for the dull late-summer plumage of many ducks?

Q7. Who created the Wildfowl Trust?

Q8. Which is bigger: Cormorant or Shag?

Q9. Of which warbler does the young have a chestnut cap?

Q10. Which two thrushes are winter visitors to Britain?

Q11. Which bird sometimes has 'Polish' young?

Q12. Whose tail is more deeply forked: Red Kite or Black Kite?

Q13. Which bird of prey is agile enough to catch Swallows?

Q14. Which is the only species of bird entirely confined to Britain?

Q15. Which has the longer bill: Black-tailed Godwit or Bar-tailed Godwit?

Q16. Which group of seabirds steals the food of others?

Q17. What is the European counterpart of the Pied Wagtail?

Q18. Which dove 'purrs'.

Q19. Which duck's feathers make the best filler for bedding?

Q20. What is Britain's wild parrot called?

Q21. What seabird did the Ancient Mariner shoot?

Q22. Which five British birds have the word 'golden' in their names?

Q23. Which thrush is a summer visitor to Britain?

Q24. Which black and white wader has an upturned bill?

Q25. Which duck has 'sails'?

Q26. Which close relative of the Chaffinch is mainly a winter visitor?

Q27. Which bird never sees its young?

Q28. Which summer visitor arrives first: the Swallow or the Swift?

Q29. What is the Bearded Reedling's more familiar name?

Q30. Which grouse turns white in winter?

Q31. Which summer visitor 'churrs' at dusk?

Q32. Which bird plasters mud round the entrance to its nest hole?

Q33. Which European queen had a falcon named after her?

Q34. Which Scoter, other than the Common Scoter, is regularly seen off our coasts in winter?

Q35. Which is the biggest owl in Europe?

Q36. Which owl calls 'tu-whit, tu-whoo'?

Q37. What looks like a tufted duck but has a grey back?

Q38. Which goose eats eel-grass?

Q39. Which crow builds a roof over its nest?

Q40. Which woodland breeder has a 'roding' display flight?

Q41. Which British martin has small white spots in the upper tail?

Q42. What is the former name of the Dunnock?

Q43. What is the British counterpart of the Blue-headed Wagtail?

Q44. Which bird makes mud nests under the eaves of house roofs?

Q45. Which is the commonest finch in Britain?

Q46. Which close relative of the Goldcrest is a rare breeder in Britain?

Q47. What bird-table bird has a white nape?

Q48. What is the usual name for the Yellow Bunting?

Q49. In what area do England's only Golden Eagles breed?

Q50. Where do Razorbills and Guillemots nest?

Q51. Where do Swifts nest?

Q52. Where is the gold on a Goldfinch?

Q53. What duck has curly tail feathers?

Q54. How can you tell male from female Great Tits?

Q55. What finch has red cheeks?

Q56. What is the difference between Redshank and Spotted Redshank in flight?

Q57. Which is Britain's biggest thrush?

Q58. Which is Britain's smallest thrush?

Q59. How do the songs of Blackbird and Song Thrush differ?

Q60. What rare breeding bird has a red tail?

Q61. Which common breeding wader is named after its leg colour?

Q62. What three breeding birds are named after their black and white plumage?

Q63. Which tern commonly breeds inland?

Q64. Which is Britain's largest gull?

PS.

47

Twitchett was paying one of his periodic visits to his nephew Eustace in Northamptonshire. One morning, he decided to take a dawn walk through some nearby woodland. Here are the notes he made.

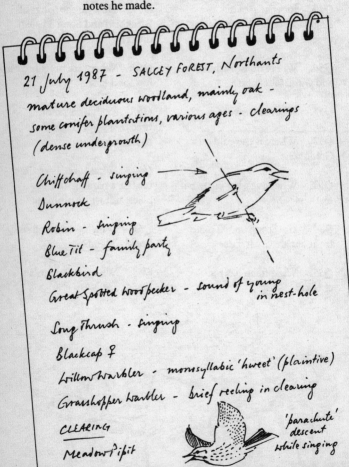

21 July 1987 - SALCEY FOREST, Northants

mature deciduous woodland, mainly oak - some conifer plantations, various ages - clearings (dense undergrowth)

Chiffchaff - singing

Dunnock

Robin - singing

Blue Tit - family party

Blackbird

Great Spotted Woodpecker - sound of young in nest-hole

Song Thrush - singing

Blackcap ♀

Willow Warbler - monosyllabic 'hweet' (plaintive)

Grasshopper Warbler - brief reeling in clearing

CLEARING

Meadow Pipit

'parachute' descent while singing

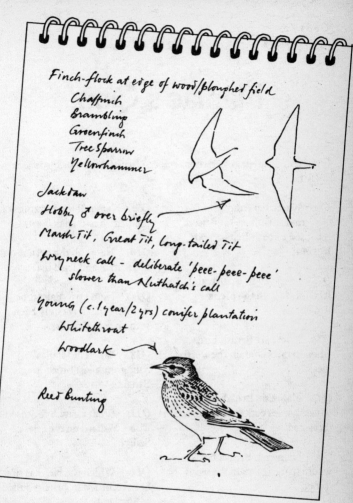

Finch-flock at edge of wood/ploughed field
  Chaffinch
  Brambling
  Greenfinch
  Tree Sparrow
  Yellowhammer

Jackdaw
Hobby ♂ over briefly
Marsh Tit, Great Tit, Long-tailed Tit
Wryneck call - deliberate 'peee-peee-peee'
    slower than Nuthatch's call

Young (c.1 year/2 yrs) conifer plantation
  Whitethroat
  Woodlark

Reed Bunting

Question: there are six unlikely or
erroneous identifications in these notes.
What are they?

Maniac's Quiz

For the dedicated: all questions refer to British birds, or birds seen in Britain.

Q1. Name ten American passerines that have only been recorded once in Britain and Ireland.

Q2. Name eight British and Irish birds with the prefix American.

Q3. Name six British birds whose names contain the word 'necked'.

Q4. Name six British birds whose names contain the word 'breasted'.

Q5. Name ten British birds whose names contain the word 'billed'.

Q6. Name ten British birds whose names contain the word 'tailed'.

Q7. Name all the swifts on the British and Irish list.

Q8. Name all the terns on the British and Irish list.

Q9. Name all the buntings on the British and Irish list.

Q10. Name all the herons on the British and Irish list.

Q11. Name two Palearctic warblers that have only been seen once in Britain.

Q12. When did Pallas' Sandgrouse last breed in Britain?

Q13. What rarity hybridised with a Mallard on the Isles of Scilly?

Q14. Which warbler has not been recorded in Britain outside of Shetland?

Q15. Where could you have seen a Black-browed Albatross in Britain in 1968?

Q16. What have Purple Heron, White Stork, Buff-breasted Sandpiper and Scarlet Rosefinch in common?

Q17. What is the difference between the under-tail coverts of Swallow and Red-rumped Swallow?

Q18. Which is the odd-one-out? Siberian Thrush, American Robin, Eye-browed Thrush, Grey-cheeked Thrush.

Q19. Place the following warblers in order of increasing rarity in Britain. Orphean, Desert, Marmora's, Ruppell's and Sardinian.

Q20. Place the following in order of increasing rarity in Britain. Broad-billed Sandpiper, Baird's Sandpiper, Great Snipe, Marsh Sandpiper and Wilson's Phalarope.

Q21. Of which rarity were more than 17,000 seen in 1980?

Q22. What species on the British list was last seen in Suffolk in 1962?

Q23. How does a juvenile Penduline Tit differ from an adult?

Q24. What new bird for Britain was seen at Blacktoft Sands, Humberside in September 1981?

Q25. What have Slender-billed Gull, Grey-rumped Sandpiper, Black Lark, Snow Finch and Masked Shrike in common?

Q26. Where was Britain's first Little Whimbrel seen?

Q27. What American passerine has only been seen once in Britain, in Dorset, in 1966?

Q28. What was the first American passerine to be seen in Britain and Ireland?

Q29. What was the first American non-passerine to be seen in Britain and Ireland?

Q30. Name eight vagrant birds of prey that have been seen in Britain in the last 50 years.

Q31. How would you distinguish a Solitary from a Green Sandpiper in flight?

Q32. How do the tails of Pallas' Grasshopper and Grasshopper Warbler differ?

Q33. Which American warbler has only been recorded once in Britain, in Scotland?

Q34. Which American warbler has only been recorded once in Britain, in Wales?

Q35. Which is the rarest of the six British birds with 'winged' in their names?

Q36. Which is the rarest of the four British birds with 'toed' in their names?

Q37. Why might you particularly visit Slimbridge in January or February?

Q38. Name the two rarest American ducks on the British list.

Q39. What rarity has only been recorded in 4 flocks, totalling 42 birds.

Q40. How many species of wheatear are there on the British list?

Q41. Which warbler has bred only once in Britain?

Q42. More than 400 of these have been seen in Britain, 315 in 1968: what are they?

Q43. How would you tell the difference between European and American races of Whimbrel?

Q44. What bred in Nottinghamshire in 1945 and attempted again in Cambridgeshire in 1984?

Q45. What last nested in Britain in Sussex in 1955?

Q46. What colour is a Ring-necked Duck's ring?

Q47. What rarity resembles a miniature Red-backed Shrike?

Q48. What American wader nested in Scotland in 1975?

Q49. What bird was first recorded on a bird table in Devon?

Q50. What bird left its mark on the trees of Tresco, Isles of Scilly in 1975?

Q51. What bird travelled to Britain with the Falklands task force?

Q52. How can you tell adult Spoonbills from juveniles in flight?

Q53. What gull attempted to breed in 1975-8 but was unsuccessful?

Q54. What is the American counterpart of the Common Gull?

Q55. Name 11 introduced species of non-passerines on the British list.

Q56. What pipit is identified by its simple 'pwit' call?

Q57. How many gulls on the British list have black heads in breeding plumage?

Q58. Where have the most new records for Britain and Ireland been seen?

Q59. Place the following buntings in order of increasing rarity in Britain: Black-headed, Little, Ortolan, Rustic, Yellow-breasted.

Q60. Place the following wheatears in order of increasing rarity in Britain: Black, Black-eared, Desert, Isabelline, Pied.

Q61. *Petrosus, spinoletta* and *rubescens* were once all one species. What are they now called?

Q62. What was first recorded in Warwickshire in 1975?

Q63. What has only been recorded twice in Britain, on Fair Isle in 1905 and 1981?

Q64. What colonist from North Africa was first recorded in Suffolk in 1971.

I havn't a clue what it is – but as long as it is bringing us food, I think we had better humour it !!

P.S.

The Near Thing

It had been an unusually fine day, and, being Saturday, the bar of the *Coot and Corncrake* was full. The air was full of happy anticipation of the next day's birdwatching. 'Could well be a few Pallas's around tomorrow' opined a barbour and green wellingtons in the corner; 'and even a Radde's or a Dusky' added his track-suited companion. Over by the window, two green anoraks were engaged in excited conversation. 'That Red-throated Pipit today puts me up to 399' one of them was saying; 'I'm still missing a Pechora – if one of those turned up tomorrow, it would make the round 400.'

Over in his accustomed seat, Twitchett pricked up his ears. 'Ah, the Pechora', he said with a chuckle. 'Perhaps I should get my nephew Billy along. As far as I know, he still hasn't got a Pechora. Have I told you' he asked reaching for his pipe ' about my nephew Billy and the Pechora? It was a dashed near thing, I can tell you. It all began when...'

But, before his pipe was properly alight, he was rudely interrupted.

'... when your nephew Billy fell in love' intoned Stringwell in a heard-it-all-before voice.

'... and actually got to the doors of the church' continued Stickler in a similar tone.

'... and was only rescued at the last minute by the telegram.' Listman rounded off. ' "Come at once stop Pechora sighted in Girdle Ness stop plane leaves twelve fifteen", if I remember.'

'Yes, it was the last straw, poor fellow.' said Twitchett with only mild regret at being deprived of the opportunity for reminiscence. 'Months of missed rarities, cancelled birding weekends, continual absences from the pub, and nothing but a lifetime of nappy-changing and slippers in front of the fire to look forward to. He was lucky the Pechora arrived when it did, even though he got there too late, and it had gone by the time he arrived.'

'Hardly surprising seeing that it was you who sent the telegram, and the Pechora was never there in the first place' said Listman.

'Still, I suppose one should feel sorry for the girl.' His companions seemed to find this rather a strange idea.

'Why?' asked Stickler, puzzled.

'Not really' said Twitchett. 'Much better that way. It's odd, but women don't really understand that sort of thing. Something to do with the female brain, I've always thought. It was easier in my father's day, of course, when women knew their place. My mother would no more have dreamed of stopping my father going off birding whenever he wanted to than my father would have dreamed of letting her. But women today are a very different kettle of fish. Ettie – that was my nephew Billy's fiancée – actually stopped him going to see a Red-necked Nightjar on one occasion because some blasted schoolfriend of hers was having a dinner party, and she wouldn't let him take his annual trip to the Isles of Scilly for the migrants because she wanted to go shopping for *curtain materials* for their new flat.' For a moment, Twitchett seemed lost for words.

Stringwell too, seemed to have an unhappy experience to relate. 'My uncle', he said, 'had to give it up altogether when he got married. My aunt threatened to accompany him wherever he went, and to take up birdwatching herself. He simply couldn't face it. He took up law instead and became a rich and successful barrister, with six children. He used to say that he didn't miss birdwatching at all, but you could tell it wasn't true. Somehow, the zest had gone out of his life.'

For a moment, all four sat silently, pondering on the cruel fate that could wrest a man from his birdwatching.

'Ah well!' sighed Twitchett eventually. 'At least it's not likely to happen to any of us. And it must be your round by now Listman. Mine's a pint.'

While Listman disappeared into the throng at the bar, the others returned to the subject of the weekend's birdwatching. Stickler was studying an analysis of their chances the next day, which Listman had left on the table.

'According to this' he said 'there's actually a one-in-fifty chance of a Pechora turning up, given the time of year and the prevailing winds', he announced, 'although sampling error might reduce that to one-in-a-hundred. And the chances of one or more Olive-backed Pipits being seen are over fifty per cent. Over the last ten years, there have been no fewer than fifteen sightings between the tenth and sixteenth of October, with a significantly increased probability in fine weather. Furthermore... ' As he droned on, Twitchett became increasingly impatient.

'Where on earth has Listman got to?' he demanded. 'A man could die of thirst in this place.' He glanced angrily around the bar.

'Good gracious; he's talking to the colonel. What on earth is he doing that for.?'

Stringwell and Stickler both turned to look for themselves at this extraordinary sight. Twitchett appeared to be right. They could hear the colonel holding forth '... hundred and ten before lunch – or was it after tea – no, that was Trumper – and anyway... umpire... blighters... hanging too good for them... ', but what was remarkable was the sight of Listman. He was holding four pints of beer at an increasingly acute angle, spilling a trickle of liquid down the one leg he seemed to be standing on, and his face wore an expression rather like that of a dead cod on a fishmonger's slab.

At the sound of Twitchett's thundered 'Get a move on Listman', he suddenly came to. He put his other foot down with a jerk, sloshing beer over it liberally, and hurried over to the table. As he moved away, they saw for the first time that the colonel had a companion – a young and extremely pretty girl.

'Ar!' said Listman. 'Er... um... sorry about that. The colonel's got his... er... niece staying with him for the weekend, and seemed anxious that she should have a bit of company. So I thought I had better... er... ' He turned and beckoned. After gesticulating briefly to the colonel, the girl walked over to their table. The anoraks and the barbour paused briefly in their conversation as their eyes followed her progress across the room. 'Angela' said Listman, with a hint of a stammer in his voice, 'meet Twitchett, Stickler and Stringwell; you chaps, meet Angela.'

'How d'you do?' said Twitchett.

'Hi' said Stickler.

'Hello' said Stringwell.

'How nice to meet you' said Angela, with a charming smile. 'My uncle has told me so much about you, although I'm not quite clear whether you're all cricketers or birdwatchers.'

An awkward silence greeted these exchanges. Twitchett cleared his throat noisily, and took a large gulp from his mug.

'Angela is staying with the colonel for a few days', explained Listman. 'She's his uncle. No... I mean, he's her niece... er'

'That's nice' said Stickler.

'Yes' agreed Stringwell.

'Doing any sight-seeing?' enquired Twitchett.

'Well, no. I don't think I've really got time', said the girl. 'You see, I'm supposed to be going to America in a week or so's time. I've been offered rather a good job out there. I don't really want to take it, but' she smiled in an apologetic fashion 'there doesn't seem to be much to keep me here. I might just as well go – so really I ought to be doing some shopping.'

'Shopping!' repeated Twitchett. He glanced at Stringwell and Stickler in the manner of one whose worst fears have been confirmed. 'Well, that should be fun.'

In the background, the voice of the colonel was droning on. 'Never could cope with a googly... sepoys not much better... whites of their eyes... '. He seemed oblivious of the fact that he had entirely lost his audience.

'I had better get back to my uncle' said Angela. 'Although he seems to be doing quite well without me'.

'See you again' said Listman as he watched her retreating back. 'I hope' he added rather forlornly.

'Shopping!' said Twitchett with withering scorn. 'What did I tell you. Now, where were we?'

'Billy Twitchett' said Listman. It wasn't clear whether he was answering the question or just musing to himself. He seemed rather distant. 'And your phony telegram. I wonder if he really is happy now.'

'No, no, no' roared Twitchett. 'That was ages ago. Before you started mooning over that female. No, we were talking about the prospects for tomorrow. Now I have a feeling that... '

Before long, they were all settled in their chairs again, arguing cheerfully over what might or might not appear the next day: around them, the merry and comforting sound of a collection of birders in full cry. All too soon, they heard the voice of Rossie calling out 'Time ladies and gentlemen please. May I have your glasses now' and the evening was at an end.

'Good night all,' said Twitchett. 'Want a lift, Listman?'

'No thanks' said Listman. 'It's such a nice evening. I think I'll walk. Good night chaps. See you all tomorrow.'

But he didn't see them next day. Nor on Monday, nor on Tuesday. By Thursday, his companions were getting alarmed. 'You don't think he's ill?' asked Stickler. 'It'll thoroughly mess up our weekend in Suffolk if he is.'

'I don't think so' replied Stringwell. 'I'm sure I saw him early this morning. I was off for an hour or two on the marsh – jolly good session, by the way, several Curlew Sandpipers, an adult Little Stint, an immature Blue-headed Wagtail and a couple of Hobbys – and I saw him heading off the wrong way through the village. It was either him or that strange bearded fellow who was hanging around earlier on. Can't think where he was going. But don't worry. No power on earth would make Listman miss our Suffolk weekend.'

'I wouldn't be so sure of that' said Twitchett grimly. 'I've just begun to realise something. You see, I thought I saw him the other morning, just like you Stringwell – I assume you got the Pectoral

Sandpiper, by the way – but I decided it couldn't be him, partly because it seemed more likely to be the peculiar bearded fellow, who was out that morning as well, but mainly because I could see no reason for him to be heading in that direction in the first place. But you know who lives up there, don't you.'

Incomprehension was plain on the other's faces. 'No' they said.

There's only one house up there' said Twitchett, 'and it belongs to the colonel.'

Realisation dawned. Stringwell and Stickler looked aghast. 'You don't think... ' stuttered Stringwell. 'You can't mean... ' groaned Stickler.

'Yes!' said Twitchett. 'Listman has fallen in love.'

'I'm afraid it's true' said a voice from behind them. All three whirled round in unison, mouths open with surprise. Standing at the doorway of the pub, looking sheepish but defiant, was Listman. He was carrying what appeared to be the fleece of a small black sheep, and was plucking nervously at some odd wisps of hair that seemed to be glued to his shin.

'But you can't have' said Stickler feebly, 'what about Suffolk?'

'That's what I came to tell you this evening' said Listman. 'I'm afraid I won't be able to come. Awfully sorry and all that, but I'm sure you'll find someone to take my place. The thing is, Angela wants to go to London to look at carpets for the flat we want to buy; she really does have very good taste in that sort of thing. We've already got fabric for the curtains, but the local shops... '

Twitchett, Stringwell and Stickler stared in amazement as Listman babbled on. None of them seemed able to speak. Listman was chattering about electric kettles by the time that Twitchett had pulled himself together sufficiently to protest.

'For heaven's sake, Listman, do you realise what you're saying? You can't seriously be thinking of getting married.'

'Oh, but I am' said Listman 'it's all arranged. Angela has cancelled her trip to America and we're getting married next week, in the registry office. I'd invite you fellows to the reception if I could, but we're only having a few old friends of Angela's and then we're off to Paris for a few days' honeymoon.'

'Paris!' spluttered Twitchett. 'You can't imagine that you're going to see anything of interest in Paris! Suffolk is the place to be at this time of year. Think again, Listman, it's still not too late. Cancel this awful business while you still have the chance. It'll ruin your birding career. You'll never be the same man again.' It sounded almost as though he were begging, and certainly there was no mistaking his terrible earnestness. If ever a man was sincere, it was Twitchett. Even Listman was touched.

'I know' he said apologetically. 'Believe me it wasn't easy. But when Angela smiles, it just does something to me. My knees go all rubbery and there's a hollow ache in the pit of my stomach...'

'Your usual Sunday morning hangover, you mean' interjected Stringwell, but Listman was not to be deterred.

'... and I knew as soon as I saw her that she was the only girl for me. I realised of course, that I would have to give up birdwatching – you can't ask a girl to understand something like that – so I have had to pretend that I'm really not interested at all. Jolly hard it's been sometimes, I can tell you. I could have sworn a Lesser Short-toed Lark flew overhead calling the other day – Angela even pointed it out and asked what it was – but I fought the urge to dash after it with the binoculars and told her that I thought it was probably a sparrow.'

Twitchett uttered a groan and put his head in his hands, Stickler's eyes bulged with disbelief and Stringwell looked as though he were about to cry.

'But I feel better for it' Listman continued, looking distinctly virtuous. 'It is a far better thing that I do now than I have ever done. What more can a man want than the love of a good woman? I shan't really miss birding after a while. Anyway...'

'In that case', demanded Twitchett severely, 'what were you doing out on the marsh wearing that hideous false beard?'

'Who, me?' asked Listman, hastily stuffing the sheep's fleece into his pocket, and pulling a few more wisps of hair from his chin. 'No, no. You must be thinking of someone else.' He attempted a careless laugh, but the result came out as a cracked and hysterical giggle. He surveyed the unbelieving faces in front of him, and gave up. 'Oh all right' he said, and slumped into his usual chair. He had a drawn and anxious expression. 'Yes, it was me. I just thought I'd take a quick look round – for old times sake, you know. But *please* don't tell Angela about this. I really will give it up soon... er... tomorrow, in fact.'

His friends looked sceptically at each other. 'Two-timing her already?' asked Stickler, sarcastically. 'Well you had better improve your disguise in future. The marriage won't last a minute if she ever sees you wearing that overgrown fungus.'

'Try borrowing one of Twitchett's old suits' suggested Stringwell. 'You'd be safe in one of them. Nobody can bear to look at them; even strong men avert their eyes.'

Listman was not amused. 'Very funny' he said. 'I've made up my mind. I'm marrying Angela, and that's that'. He squared his shoulders resolutely. 'I can feel the urge dying out already. Anyway, I must be off now. We're supposed to be going to a jolly little dinner party with one of Angela's school friends, and I'd better not be late. I don't suppose I shall be seeing quite so much of you chaps in the future, so... ' he hesitated, 'well, thanks for everything. I'll miss you' and he was gone.

For several minutes, nobody spoke. There was little to be heard in the bar except for the dull chink of shove-ha'pennies in a far corner and the sound of the colonel snoring gently in his usual seat by the bar. It was Rossie who broke the silence. 'Last orders' he yelled.

'Good Lord', said Twitchett, suddenly galvanised into activity. He drained his pint. 'Come on you lot', he said, 'drink up', and, seizing their empty glasses, he strode rapidly to the bar. 'Four of the usual he said. Hadn't realised it was so late. We've all had a nasty shock.' Just then, the pub clock started to chime. Twitchett glanced at it idly, and then suddenly rounded on Rossie. 'Here,' he said angrily 'it's only ten o'clock. What's all this about last orders'.

'So it is' said Rossie blandly. 'Well, you hadn't ordered a drink for at least an hour. I've got to make a living somehow. And I take it you only wanted three?'

Twitchett decided against further remonstration; there were more important things to discuss. 'Look' he said as he returned to his chair. 'We've got to do something about this. Somebody must have some ideas. Come on you two, think!'

'Perhaps we could kidnap him?' suggested Stickler.

'Try not to be more of an idiot than you already are' said String-well coldly. 'What about you Twitchett. What on earth is the use of all those uncles, cousins and aunts of yours if they can't help solve a simple problem like this?'

'I've been trying to think of someone. But there's only Billy, and his telegram, and Listman would never fall for that one. He knows all about it already. And I don't think my great uncle Dreyfus's solution would help – he is supposed to have tarred and feathered his best friend's fiancée; it made a sensation at the local assizes.'

'I think we've all had too much of a shock to think of anything just at the moment' said Stickler. 'I suggest we take a day or two to consider the problem. I take it that we will have to cancel – or rather postpone – the weekend in Suffolk?' The others murmured reluctant assent. 'So why don't we meet here again on Saturday, and pool our ideas then.'

Twitchett was the first to arrive on Saturday evening. When the other two arrived a few minutes later, they found him already stretched out in his chair. 'Sit down' he boomed. 'Time to make plans. Now what I think is this... '

But he got no further. For at that moment, the door of the pub burst open, and in came an extremely pretty girl. It turned out to be Angela. She walked across to Twitchett's table. She had plainly been crying, and even now seemed only just in control of herself.

'Where's Willy?' she demanded. They looked at her nonplussed.

'Willy?, Willy who?'

'Why, Willy of course, you know, Willy Listman.' Twitchett, Stickler and Stingwell looked at each other with wild surmise. The thought that Listman might have a christian name was novel enough; but that it should be Willy... Stickler began to giggle.

'No idea' said Twitchett, regarding Angela with the sort of look that Hercules might have given the Medusa's locks. 'I'd have thought you would have known. Why? Have you lost him?'

'Oh! It's all so terrible' sobbed Angela, subsiding into what used to be Listman's chair. 'There's been this terrible misunderstanding. I see now that our marriage could never have worked. But I really did think when I met him that he was a keen birdwatcher. I see now that my uncle must have meant keen cricketer, but he did seem to be talking so earnestly to you all about birds that evening in here and I was sure that he was just the sort of man I wanted to spend my life with.'

Twitchett seemed to be choking on his beer. 'There, there' he coughed. 'You mustn't get so upset. Tell us what all this is about.'

Angela seemed a little more composed. 'My father' she began 'is Eugene Wangler, author of *Identification problems of the Holarctic Treecreepers* and several other ornithological classics, and I have been brought up with a love of birds since I was knee-high to a grasshopper. The only problem was that I never seemed to meet anyone who shared my passion. My father made enough money from the royalties of his books to give me an expensive private education – you know, finishing school, university and all that sort of thing – but all I ever met were people who were going to be prime ministers, or Lord this that or the other, or film stars or millionaires. Not one of them ever wanted to spend a day or two ringing buntings, or studying the eating habits of the larger waders. I was nearly in despair. So I vowed that I would marry the first man I met who really loved and knew about birds. I knew that we could share a happy and fruitful life together and, if we ever had children, we could teach them all about birds as well. When I met Willy.. ' Twitchett, Stickler and Stringwell all winced silently '... I thought I had found the man I was looking for.'

'It was only after we were formally engaged that I began to have doubts. I think it was the Lesser Short-toed Lark that first worried me. When I pointed it out to him overhead and asked him what it was (I thought he would easily get the answer), he told me he

61

thought it was a sparrow! He didn't even rush out with his binoculars to follow it. And when I casually mentioned Suffolk to him, he hastily said something about never wanting to visit the place again, and he really ought to have known that now is much the best time to pay it a visit. So I decided that I would have to give him one last chance. I devised a little test for him. If he had passed it, I would have been planning my trousseau now. But he didn't. He failed. So now I'm going to America after all. In fact, I'm on my way to the station this very minute to catch the train to the airport, I shall never see him again. I just thought I should let him know. We Wanglers do not lack courage.' She concluded forlornly.

Twitchett was having difficulty finding his voice. 'Terrible' he said eventually. 'Still, that's life. It all goes to show. One should never jump to hasty decisions about people. All's well that ends well. Much better that you should find out now.' He petered out. There didn't seem to be much more to be said. 'Well, my dear. Better not miss your plane. Hope you enjoy America. Big place, if I remember. And bon voyage. We'll pass the message on to er... Willy, never fear, and we'll make sure he doesn't take it too hard. By the way', he asked as Angela got up to go. 'What precisely was this little test you devised?'

'It was this' she said, digging into her coat pocket. She handed some scraps of torn paper to Twitchett. 'It was just that I wanted to think of something that I knew no real birdwatcher could resist. So I sent him this. I'd told him I wanted to go shopping this weekend, so I knew he wasn't doing anything important. He could easily have gone if he'd wanted to. But when I went to his house this morning, I found him muttering with rage, and tearing my test into small pieces. Here, you have them. I don't want them any more.' She dropped the scraps of paper into Twitchett's hand, and left.

'Phew!' said Twitchett. 'Now there's a turn up for the book. What on earth can all this be about?' He pieced together the various scraps of paper, until what was apparently a 'telemessage' took shape. 'You won't believe this' he said, as he spread the jigsaw out on the table. He began to laugh, a triumphant surge of uproarious noise. 'Listman certainly didn't.'

Stickler and Stringwell craned their necks to see the document. 'Come at once' they read. 'Pechora sighted on Fair Isle. Plane leaves eleven forty-five.'

Questions. *1*. What sort of birds are the barbour and green wellingtons discussing? 2. What did Stringwell misidentify on the marsh? *3*. The Pectoral Sandpiper was later discovered to be something much rarer. What?

QUESTION TIME

Word Play

All the questions in this quiz should be easy for crossword enthusiasts. The first 32 each contain a 'cryptic' clue to a bird's name, followed by a factual reference to some aspect of the bird's appearance, habitat, distribution or behaviour. The second 32 are all anagrams – a pencil and a piece of paper are recommended. The number of letters in the answer is given after each question.

Cryptic clues.

Q1. Got one's teeth into a seabird in the reeds (7).

Q2. Second letter wandering – in winter (9).

Q3. Sounds like a busy bee – or a cat? (7).

Q4. Cost of a close shave on the cliffs (9).

Q5. Dark and stormy – but still singing (11).

Q6. Get up, pussy, in a crowded colony (9).

Q7. Is back to hide at bird tables in winter (6).

Q8. Heavy garden implement, mainly on the continent (6).

Q9. Accept as true summer visitor (7).

Q10. Apivorous as well as colourful (8).

Q11. Tie up boat to female with colourful bill (7).

Q12. Fancy, British Rail taking its last with a striped crown (8).

Q13. Big in the sky and below the surface (6).

Q14. Ride this horse for an obsessive catcher of House Martins (5).

Q15. Rub down market at home in a tunnel (4,6).

Q16. Determination to have offspring's fuel, following ships at sea (7,6).

Q17. Union ban on 'plane makes a scavenger (5,4).

Q18. Sounds like half of a child's train is black (6).

Q19. Dwelling place for a boxing bout before the argument, introduced worldwide (5,7).

Q20. Initially tenth and takes eggs (3).

Q21. Orb of precious metal found in box (9).

Q22. Dash about side of building with white in wing (7).

Q23. Cabbage, for example, with some yarn about Scottish flows (10).

Q24. Husky measure is one of the commonest (9).

Q25. Surgeon's street with one of five northern duck (9).

Q26. Marine reptile dived in the States, and purrs (6,4).

Q27. Brown gets nothing back and is commonest on the coast (6).

Q28. Weighty talk with black-headed male (9).

Q29. Italian river, becoming oceanic with a sound like a meat truss, returns along the coast on passage (8,4).

Q30. Northerner and Queen, after fabric, gather at sea (6,6).

Q31. Cut off point from the marshes (5).

Q32. Increase the flying apparatus with a crest (7).

Anagrams

Q33. Serin gland (10).

Q34. Damn rain (8).

Q35. Hat trouble (10).

Q36. Clear ice pail (12).

Q37. Selling a bus (7,4).

Q38. Spread preening (5,9).

Q39. Tie tipper (4,5).

Q40. Real happy ogre (4,9).

Q41. A thin niggle (11).

Q42. Raffle die (9).

Q43. Carved old leo (8,4).

Q44. Crack Nero (9).

Q45. Our greeds (3,6).

Q46. Treason tree (7,4).

Q47. Cheesy tractor (13).

Q48. Remelts port (5,6).

Q49. Lose other draw (5-5,3).

Q50. Argue task (5,4).

Q51. Letter bilge (6,5).

Q52. South marine (5,6).

Q53. Rat wailer (5,4).

Q54. Brute ending (4,7).

Q55. Shark lore (5,4).

Q56. Extra man washer (4,10).

Q57. Dotty clasp fetcher (7,10).

Q58. Avert odd ditherer (3-8,5).

Q59. Battered Di (7,3).

Q60. A grey nag (8).

Q61. Drew large barn (6,7).

Q62. Rye hiker stagger (5,4,6).

Q63. Rents unto (9).

Q64. Pen driver log (6,6).

From the Archives.

Those who frequent the *Coot and Corncrake* will no doubt be aware that there has been, from time to time, considerable speculation as to the origin of the pub' and the extent of its antiquity. The landlord's claim that the present sign, and thus the name itself, is derived from Plantagenet times, is generally greeted with scepticism. The editors, have now found, quite by chance, some correspondence in the Publisher's archives which appears to shed some light on this matter. Regrettably, as is often the case with this Publisher's archives, the correspondence is not only incomplete, but mutilated as well. The little that remains is reproduced here.

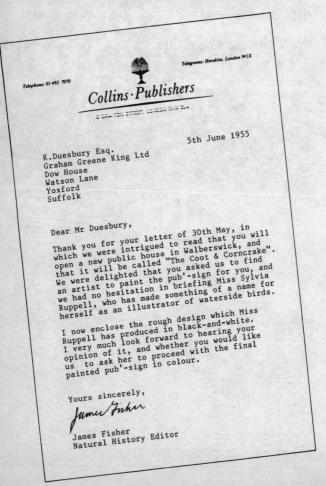

Telegrams: Herakles, London W1X

Telephone: 01-493 7070

Collins · Publishers

8 GRAFTON STREET, LONDON W1X 3LA

5th June 1955

K.Duesbury Esq.
Graham Greene King Ltd
Dow House
Watson Lane
Yoxford
Suffolk

Dear Mr Duesbury,

Thank you for your letter of 30th May, in which we were intrigued to read that you will open a new public house in Walberswick, and that it will be called "The Coot & Corncrake". We were delighted that you asked us to find an artist to paint the pub'-sign for you, and we had no hesitation in briefing Miss Sylvia Ruppell, who has made something of a name for herself as an illustrator of waterside birds.

I now enclose the rough design which Miss Ruppell has produced in black-and-white. I very much look forward to hearing your opinion of it, and whether you would like us to ask her to proceed with the final painted pub'-sign in colour.

Yours sincerely,

James Fisher

James Fisher
Natural History Editor

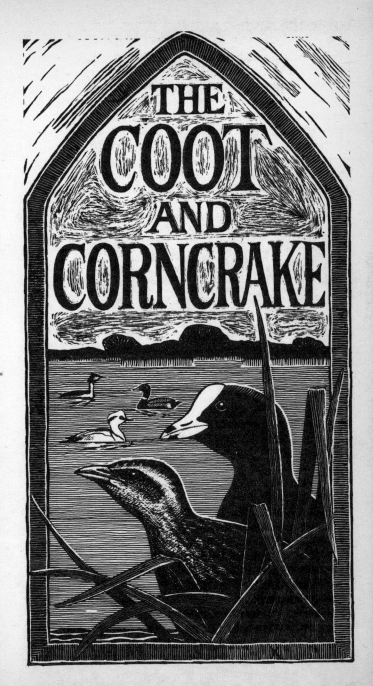

THE COOT AND CORNCRAKE

GRAHAM GREENE KING LTD
BREWERS and WINE MERCHANTS

James Fisher Esq.   June 20th 1955
Natural History Editor
Collins Publishers
14 St James's Place
London S.w.1

Dear Mr Fisher,

The "Coot & Corncrake", Walberswick

Thank you for your letter of 5th June, and for all
the trouble you are taking in helping us to launch
our new public house successfully. Miss Ruppell's
design for the sign is quite excellent, and we
should now like formally to commission her to
paint the final, hanging, double-sided panel in
full colour. We would propose a fee of five gns
for her work, and trust that Miss Ruppell will
deem this to be a satisfactory remuneration.

Before she proceeds, however, we would like you to
draw to her attention two errors which our experts
tell us exist in the design which she has made in
black-and-white.

First, the
not the

Note: the brewery no longer exists: Sylvia Ruppell cannot be found.
Nobody at Collins can remember the details of what happened over
30 years ago.

Can *you* identify Sylvia Ruppell's two errors, which Mr Duesbury
presumably described in the part of his letter that was at some time
torn off?

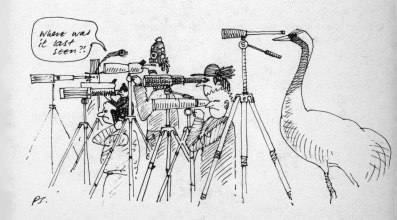

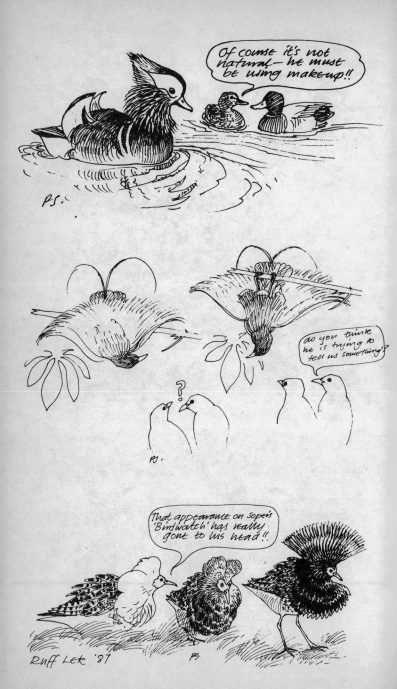

QUESTION
TIME

My Name Begins With

One of the favourite pastimes for a cold winter evening in the *Coot and Corncrake* is the game 'My name begins with…' The rules are simple. Each player thinks of a bird and then makes a (true) statement about it. As an additional clue, he (or possibly she) announces the initial letter of the bird's name; if the name consists of two or more words, the letter refers to the first of them. All the answers to the following clues are British birds.

Q1. I'm on the up-and-up in a roundabout way – and my name begins with T.

Q2. I'm often in a spin – and my name begins with G.

Q3. I'm no longer in England – and my name begins with C.

Q4. I am an Asian immigrant – and my name begins with C.

Q5. I keep my mouth shut – and my name begins with M.

Q6. I'm a squealer – and my name begins with W.

Q7. I enjoy my trips – and my name begins with D.

Q8. My big relative towers above me – and my name begins with J.

Q9. I travel the furthest – and my name begins with A.

Q10. I'm high spirited – and my name begins with S.

Q11. I stoop to conquer – and my name begins with P.

Q12. I'm a drum major – and my name begins with G.

Q13. I sing with many keys – and my name begins with C.

Q14. My business is booming – and my name begins with B.

Q15. My solo arrival is proverbial – and my name begins with S.

Q16. I often roost in urban flocks – and my name begins with P.

Q17. I have a small task – and my name begins with L.

Q18. I live in a burrow – and my name begins with P.

Q19. I've always got a muddy front door – and my name begins with N.

Q20. I'm really laughing in Latin – and my name begins with B.

Q21. I always laugh – and my name begins with G.

Q22. I always warn you when I fly away – and my name begins with R.

Q23. I fly silently – and my name begins with B.

Q24. I'm Black in America – and my name begins with C.

Q25. I'll have a White Shield – and my name begins with C.

Q26. I'm the largest percher – and my name begins with R.

Q27. I'm louder than I look – and my name begins with W.

Q28. I've been round Brazil – and my name begins with N.

Q29. I've recently gone nuts – and my name begins with S.

Q30. I walk on a bed – and my name begins with D.

Q31. I display nightly – and my name begins with W.

Q32. I appear like clockwork – and my name begins with C.

Q33. I'm heard but not seen – and my name begins with C.

Q34. I have more behind than in front – and my name begins with L.

Q35. Despite my name I have a tail – and my name begins with M.

Q36. I'm good at impersonations – and my name begins with S.

Q37. I'm sometimes blue – and my name begins with S.

Q38. I'm a little down in the mouth – and my name begins with W.

Q39. I'm always whistling – and my name begins with W.

Q40. I 'whinny' until I'm hoarse – and my name begins with L.

Q41. I've got a sweet tooth – and my name begins with H.

Q42. I eat a lot of fish – and my name begins with G.

Q43. I eat fish but I don't catch them – and my name begins with G.

Q44. I'm really a moor hen – and my name begins with R.

Q45. I have another name like my call – and my name begins with L.

Q46. I try to turn the tide – and my name begins with K.

Q47. I run along The Strand – and my name begins with S.

Q48. I'm big game – and my name begins with P.

Q49. I've got a black mark for my cheek – and my name begins with T.

Q50. I'm good at spelling – and my name begins with M.

Q51. I'm under Eve's care – and my name begins with H.

Q52. I repeat myself – and my name begins with S.

Q53. I look better than I sound – and my name begins with R.

Q54. I'm a hoot – and my name begins with T.

Q55. I'm not welcome at fish farms – and my name begins with G.

Q56. I blanch at the thought of winter – and my name begins with P.

Q57. You can always follow my movements – and my name begins with R.

Q58. I'm not wild about towns – and my name begins with R.

Q59. I don't only come from Kent – and my name begins with S.

Q60. I now need no introduction – and my name begins with L.

Q61. I bear a family crest – and my name begins with S.

Q62. I probe deeply – and my name begins with S.

Q63. Flying is my life – and my name begins with S.

Q64. I build tunnels – and my name begins with S.

Spring on Fetlar; Shetland Isles...

74

Twitchett Snaps

A small crowd was gathered around the far wall of the bar of the *Coot and Corncrake* where the social events noticeboard had once been. The board had now gone, due in part to the disgraceful dismissal of the domino team's captain for cheating (he had been caught painting on extra spots) but mostly to the demise of the darts team. The pub team, which was made up mainly of birders, had been playing an away match against the *Saracen's Head*. During the match it was discovered that the only genuine Saracen playing, the son of a local rich Arab, had darts flights specially made from Houbara Bustard feathers. The show of anger from the birders brought protestations from him that the unfortunate bird in question had at least been caught by a Scottish Peregrine and this served only to fuel their fury, culminating in an all-out fight. Twitchett and the rest of the Coot's darts team were thenceforth banned from the league for a season, not so much for their unruly behaviour but because of what they did to the Saracen's darts captain who objected to what was done to him with a pair of ringing pliers.

In place of the noticeboard there was now a collection of photographs of rare birds for people to identify. The twenty pictures were changed monthly and an inevitably alcoholic prize was awarded to the first person to identify both the bird and the locality of each photo. Twitchett and his friends were, of course, in charge of selecting the pictures. Rossie, like all good landlords, had recognised the potential of photos like these, and now had a thriving side-line selling pictures of rarities on behalf of a rapidly growing number of photographers. Anyone could ask for 'The Album' and order copies of the hundred or so pictures inside.

Twitchett watched the crowd by the board and shook his head sadly. 'Look at them, Stringwell' he said. 'They're all looking at the board and none of them realise what's just above it.' He was, of course, referring to one of the many glass cases dotted around the bar on high, dusty shelves. The cases all contained stuffed birds which, with their unrecognisably faded feathers, bore few traces of their former glory. The specimen above the board formed the basis of one of Twitchett's favourite stories about his great-grandfather Peregrine. The bird was one of the so-called 'Halstead Rarities' for which Peregrine was rightly infamous. It represented Britain and Ireland's first record of an Acadian Flycatcher. It was caught by Peregrine on a 'Murdoch's Butcher' while he was trout fishing on a small stream in south west Ireland. The record was accepted at first until a detailed investigation showed that the fly it was caught on bore no resemblance to anything in its natural diet. Twitchett, when he told the tale, was always adamant that the record was genuine. 'It is a well known fact' he would bellow 'that vagrants frequently change their diets. After all we all eat kebabs when we visit Greece and spaghetti in Italy, so why shouldn't a flycatcher go for a different fly. A 'Murdoch's Butcher' looks quite tasty to me...'

But today Twitchett was not telling this tale, he was watching the people at the noticeboard which held details of the *Coot and Corncrake* Photographic Competition. Professional bird photographers were excluded, and this included all who had their work in 'The Album'. Photographs had to be opportunistic and could not involve lengthy preparations with hides and so the competition's subject was rarities. The Pictures had to be taken during the month of May, which would be starting in three weeks. Prizes would be awarded for the Best Rare Bird photograph; the best set of five rarity photos and finally the Rarest Bird category. The competition was sponsored by the twitcher's magazine 'Dipping-in' which would be providing prizes and featuring a selection of the entries. Entries had to be submitted by the end of the first week in June and would be judged by a panel of four. Twitchett was intially rather upset at not being asked to be a judge, but eventually decided that he preferred looking at real birds to photos.

One of the people studying the board with close attention was 'Snapper' Snodgrass. Twitchett had first encountered him on an autumn holiday on the isles of Scilly. An Ovenbird was discovered on St Agnes and a crowd of about 150 people were waiting patiently for it to appear. After half an hour it was seen briefly and it was another twenty minutes before it came out into the open. More than 300 eyes focused on the bird and there were sighs of appreciation. Suddenly there was a loud snapping and crashing sound as a strange figure dressed in a camouflage jacket covered in leaves fell out of a tree and onto the path where the bird was standing. A large branch and various items of photographic equipment fell with him and the bird naturally disappeared never to be seen again. Thus 'Snapper', as he came to be called, was first seen by the birding community. His photographic techniques became legendary although they often did little to endear him to other birders. Being small he was always able to get to the front of a crowd by by crawling between the legs of the birders and tripods. When a Black Vulture was seen in the New Forest he spent three days lying in the open, playing dead. He used a hollowed out log to get close to a Bufflehead on Loch Fleet and was eventually washed ashore at Tarbat Ness twelve hours later. A hollow tree was used when Britain's first Downy Woodpecker was found in Cornwall. This plan seemed promising until the bird landed on the false tree and began hammering at his lens.

One person certain to enter the competition was Twitchett's arch-rival, Gripsall, who had recently taken up photography in a big way. He had purchased the latest computerised Japanese camera made by Travolta, with a shutter action like greased lightning. A 1000 mm. mirror lens, an autowinder and some super-fast film completed his equipment.

The month of May soon arrived and the photographers were all out in force. The first rarity to appear was a Whiskered Tern at Grafham which gave everyone good shots when it dived. A Little Bittern at Leighton Moss posed half-way up a reed for a lucky handful. A Collared Pratincole hawked over people's heads at Stod-marsh, though only a few caught its chestnut underwing on cellu-loid. Nobody managed to capture the Thrush Nightingale at Spurn on film. In mid-May the real crippler turned up. One of the top female birders, Ann Skipton, found an Orphean Warbler in some bushes at Portland Bill – for months afterwards she was known as Little Orphean Annie! The bird was next seen when it was trapped in the bird observatory garden, but one of the rules of the com-petition stated that birds in the hand could not be photographed until an hour after they had been released. The warbler proved extremely elusive. Hundreds of birders descended on Portland to see it and at best were treated to a glimpse of tail feathers. 'Snapper' rather painfully disguised himself as a gorse bush to no avail. As fate would have it Gripsall was the sole person to photograph it. He had disappeared behind a bush to answer a call of nature when the bird suddenly hopped out right in front of him. By a combination of luck and willpower he managed to take one full-frame picture before it disappeared. In his excitement and joy he completely forgot his original purpose and ran out from the bush shouting 'I've got it on film.' A roar of laughter greeted him and it was only when someone shouted 'Are you sure its not overexposed?' that he realised his state of dress.

Twitchett was one of the unlucky people who never seemed to be standing by the right bush when the bird appeared... he dipped out. Naturally this delighted Gripsall who made dozens of enlarged prints of the photograph and distributed them around the town. As fast as Twitchett took them down, he put them up again. He even managed the unthinkable and placed one on full view in the bar of the *Coot and Corncrake*. When Twitchett entered and saw it, he began to shake and go red. Instead of sucking on his pipe he blew, causing a shower of smouldering tobacco and this imitation of Etna erupting was completed by a low growling sound which gradually grew into a fully-fledged roar. 'I'll fix him and his photo' he fumed. 'A quadruple Grouse please, Rossie.'

'Looks like you've already got one' Rossie replied with a smile, but Twitchett was not amused. He sat in complete silence for the next two hours, staring hard into the distance. He ignored all attempts by Listman and Stickler to get him to talk. Even their pleas for him to tell the story about the time he had seen a Needle-tailed Swift flying alongside the plane on his way to Shetland fell on deaf ears. Twitchett would not be satisfied until he had got even.

On the last weekend of May, Twitchett had a wedding to go to. His niece was getting married in Plymouth at midday on the Saturday and so, on the Friday evening, Twitchett drove down there. It was a nice wedding and at the reception afterwards Twitchett thought back to the last one he had been to. His friend Ackroyd had finally got round to marrying his long-suffering girl friend. At the reception, Twitchett had telephoned for news and heard about a Siberian Accentor at Flamborough Head. He rushed back into the room and announced it, causing all the birders to run out. Ackroyd and the assembled guests thought that this was a great joke and it was only when none of them had returned after a quarter of an hour that Ackroyd began to get worried. A quick phone call confirmed his fears and, in true twitching style, he commandeered the black Daimler, complete with white ribbons, and headed for Yorkshire. The guests were mortified but his wife, quite used to such eccentric behaviour, merely said 'He'd be impossible on the honeymoon if he didn't go for it' and proceeded to drink four bottles of champagne. Ironically the honeymoon was to Siberia.

'I'd better make a phone call myself' thought Twitchett and excused himself from the reception. Rossie answered the phone and read out a message that Listman had left for him. 'Ruby-throated Hummingbird at St Just. Third garden on the left after the turning to the airfield. Found at midday.' Armed with the details Twitchett rapidly said his goodbyes and headed off. Being fairly close, he arrived there before most of the crowds and only about fifty people were there, peering over the hedge of a small garden. The bird was feeding along a flower bed about twenty yards away, occasionally perching on a nearby willow. Its favourite flower was a Fuchsia but it approached anything red. Twitchett watched it for about ten minutes and then reached into his pocket for his pipe. He had forgotten that he was not wearing his usual birding clothes. The morning suit he had on explained the rather funny looks he had been getting. As he felt for his pipe, his hand found the small camera he had taken to the wedding and his mind suddenly flicked to Gripsall and his photo. He began to make a low rumbling noise and then suddenly he stopped and a smile appeared on his face. He tapped the shoulder of the birder next to him and said 'I wonder if you would do me a favour...'

When Twitchett walked into the *Coot and Corncrake* next day, he was smiling and whistling. No-one had seen him so happy for weeks.

'What's he so cheerful about?' asked Listman. 'Probably the hummingbird' replied Stringwell.

Twitchett was clearly bursting to tell them something but was curiously evasive.

'Wait for a few more minutes and you'll find out' he said cryptically.

Three minutes later the door of the pub opened and Gripsall walked in. Listman and Stringwell were poised to grab Twitchett, fully expecting him to go for Gripsall's throat, but he just sat there, smiling quietly.

'What's all this about?' growled Gripsall. 'I got a message to meet you here.'

'I thought you might like to see this' replied Twitchett, handing Gripsall an envelope. As he opened it Gripsall went white. He began grinding his teeth and then ripped up the envelope and its contents and stormed out.

'What was that all about?' asked Listman.

'I'll show you' replied Twitchett, reaching into his pocket and handing Listman a photo. The picture was very clear. It showed a hand holding up a red carnation, the sort you get as a buttonhole. As large as life beside it was the Ruby-throated Hummingbird, caught for an instant as it hovered there.

Written underneath it was 'Instamatic. F8. 64 ASA.'

Questions: *1*. Which of the birds 'Snapper' tried to photograph was the most unlikely vagrant? *2*. Which of the photographs of rarities mentioned would have been rejected?

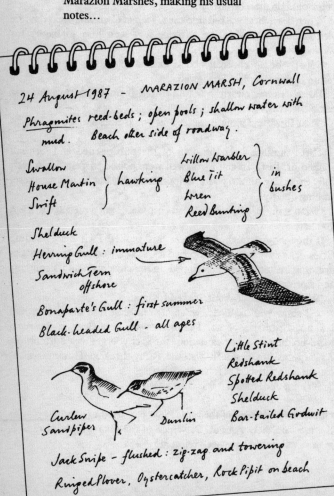

LEAVES FROM TWITCHETT'S NOTEBOOK

On an early autumn twitch to the Isles of Scilly, Twitchett took the opportunity of stopping off in Cornwall to visit Marazion Marshes, making his usual notes…

24 August 1987 – MARAZION MARSH, Cornwall

<u>Phragmites</u> reed-beds; open pools; shallow water with mud. Beach other side of roadway.

Swallow ⎫
House Martin ⎬ hawking
Swift ⎭

Willow Warbler ⎫
Blue Tit ⎪
Wren ⎬ in bushes
Reed Bunting ⎭

Shelduck
Herring Gull : immature →
Sandwich Tern offshore
Bonaparte's Gull : first summer
Black-headed Gull - all ages

Little Stint
Redshank
Spotted Redshank
Shelduck
Bar-tailed Godwit

Curlew Sandpiper   Dunlin

Jack Snipe - flushed : zig-zag and towering
Ringed Plover, Oystercatcher, Rock Pipit on beach

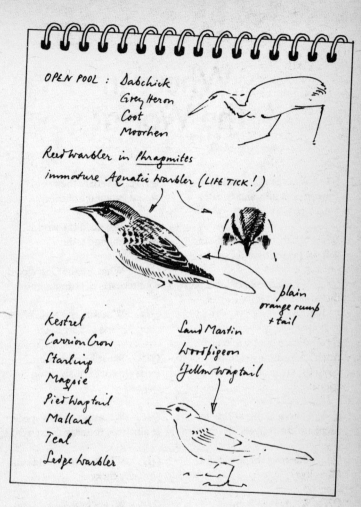

OPEN POOL : Dabchick
Grey Heron
Coot
Moorhen

Reed warbler in _phragmites_

immature Aquatic Warbler (LIFE TICK!)

plain
orange rump
+ tail

Kestrel   Sand Martin
Carrion Crow   Woodpigeon
Starling   Yellow Wagtail
Magpie
Pied Wagtail
Mallard
Teal
Sedge Warbler

Question: there are four mistakes, or
probable misidentifications in these
notes. Can you spot them?

Where in the World?

Q1. Where in the world can you see penguins and Greater Flamingos?

Q2. Where in the world can you see penguins and Coot?

Q3. Which family of birds lays the largest egg relative to its body size?

Q4. Which family of North America birds, apart from cuckoos, are nest parasites?

Q5. Where in the world did Elephant-birds live?

Q6. Where in the world did Moas live?

Q7. What is the family Paradisaeidae?

Q8. What is the family Phasianidae?

Q9. What is *Pavo cristatus* better known as?

Q10. What is *Meleagris gallopavo* better known as?

Q11. Where in the world would you find fodies?

Q12. Where in the world would you find todies?

Q13. What are the Old World counterparts of hummingbirds?

Q14. What are the New World counterparts of hornbills?

Q15. What European bird feeds almost exclusively on snakes?

Q16. Where was a new species of albatross recently discovered?

Q17. Where in the world can you see a flicker?

Q18. Where in the world can you see a vanga?

Q19. What is the world's smallest seabird?

Q20. What is the world's largest penguin?

Q21. What is *Cardinalis cardinalis*?

Q22. What is *Fregata magnificens?*

Q23. Where in the world can you see wild peacocks?

Q24. Where in the world can you see wild guineafowl?

Q25. What type of bird is a Wallace's Standardwing?

Q26. What type of bird is a tragopan?

Q27. Where do Zebra Finches come from?

Q28. What type of bird is a Cordon-bleu?

Q29. Where in the world can you see a fairy?

Q30. Where in the world can you see a Galah?

Q31. Which bird is endemic to Algeria?

Q32. Which bird is found only on Fuertaventura?

Q33. What type of birds are Jabirus and Marabous?

Q34. Name the most naturally widespread bird in the world?

Q35. Where in the world can you see a Cock of the Rock?

Q36. Where in Europe can you see a Barbary Partridge?

Q37. Name the three species of puffin in the world?

Q38. Which family of birds is unique to the Palearctic.

Q39. Which bird builds the largest communal nests?

Q40. What do Crab Plover, Painted Snipe, Ibisbill and Magellanic Plover have in common?

Q41. Where in the world can you see a Plains Wanderer?

Q42. Where in the world can you see a Rothschild's Starling?

Q43. What is *Avocetta recurvirostris?*

Q44. What are *Dacelo, Alcedo* and *Lacedo?*

Q45. What family is Pelecanoidiidae?

Q46. What do a condor, a swift and a rubythroat have in common?

Q47. Where in the world would you see a Kagu?

Q48. Where in the world would you see a Takahe?

Q49. What is the difference between *Otis* and *Otus?*

Q50. What is the difference between *Crex* and *Crax?*

Q51. Where does *Oceanites oceanicus* breed?

Q52. Where does *Nipponia nippon* breed?

Q53. Where in the world can you see an Akiapolaau?

Q54. Where in the world can you see a Coral-billed Nuthatch?

Q55. Which bird is the Sunbittern most closely related to? A heron, a cormorant or a crane?

Q56. What order of birds does the Secretary Bird belong to?

Q57. In which four European species is the female larger and more colourful than the male?

Q58. What islands are the home of a unique family of honeycreepers?

Q59. Where in the world can you see a Jabiru?

Q60. Where in the world can you see a Woodpecker Finch?

Q61. What is special about the display of bowerbirds?

Q62. What is unique about a young Hoatzin?

Q63. What family of birds do not incubate their eggs, but keep them warm under rotting vegetation?

Q64. The male of which species of bird fasts for 115 days each year?

The hazards of MIGRATION

The Channel...

European 'Sportsmen'...

Eleanoras Falcon...

the Desert...

Listless Days

It was late September and it had been a quiet autumn. Twitchett, Stringwell, Listman and Stickler were seated round the table in the *Coot and Corncrake* looking bored.

'There's bound to be something turn up soon' said Listman. 'The probability of another week going by with out a good rarity turning up is... let me see.' He took out his calculator and started punching in figures.

'Come off it Listman, we could have none at all but we know it's not likely. Working out some hypothetical figure isn't going to cheer us up' snapped Stringwell, who was amusing himself by seeing how many knots he could tie in a folded crisp packet.

Rossie came across to bring Stickler some food he had ordered. 'One Birder Burger with all the trimmings... French Bustard, Dill Piculet... made from 100 per cent Bee-eater, or was it Cattle Egret?' He surveyed the morose foursome. 'You're all looking a bit listless' he remarked, chuckling.

'You are right there, Rossie' replied Listman. 'I haven't added anything to my September list this year.'

'Come off it' snorted Stickler. 'You don't mean to tell me you keep a list for every month of the year, do you?'

'Certainly I do, and very interesting they are too. Did you know that statistically you have a greater chance of seeing more birds in October than in May, even though you can see more birds in a single day in May than in any other month. The poorest month of the year is of course July.' Listman took out a small notebook. I could get lots of ticks this month – I still need a September Little Auk and an Iceland Gull and I've never got to grips with a September Nightingale...'

'Well I think all of these lists are silly. I could never see the point of them.' stated Stickler.

'Oh yes?' said Stringwell, with a touch of sarcasm. 'So what lists do you keep?'

'Well obviously my British list and my Western Palearctic list.

My trip to the States means I've got a USA list and if you put them together that's the beginning of a world list, but that's all.'

'Don't you keep a garden list?' asked Listman.

'Well I haven't really got a garden but I do keep a sort of mental list of the birds I've seen from my window. And I suppose I've got a list of the birds on my local area, but no more. None of these stupid county lists and month lists.'

'If you think those are silly you should hear about some other lists people keep' said Twitchett. 'I know someone who keeps a TV list. He's got three video recorders to tape things when he's out and I think his list stands somewhere near two thousand. Of course, he watches all of the nature programmes for most of his birds and he's even got the extinct Laysan Island Rail on his list. He always claims that some of the best ones were seen when you would least expect them. He added twenty new birds watching news reports from the Falklands war. A few weeks ago he says there was a clip of a Rusty-cheeked Scimitar Babbler used in a video for the Rabid Bats' new single on 'Top of the Pops'. He's now saving up for a satellite dish to start a world TV list. He claims that it's cheaper than travelling to see them.'

'Well I know someone with an airport list' offered Stickler,' and then there's that strange fellow who keeps a car list, birds he has hit that is.'

'Just like train-spotting' mused Stringwell. 'They didn't have all these lists in the old days. I bet your great grandfather didn't keep lists, Twitchett.'

'It's funny you should mention old Peregrine' said Twitchett, taking out his pipe and settling into his familiar relaxed position, gently nudging his empty glass while reaching for the ashtray. Listman took the hint and went off to get a fresh round of drinks. Twitchett contentedly set about lighting his pipe.

'I did find one list amongst his diaries that I think will amuse you. It was rather a short one. Only about fifteen birds on it as I remember. There were some common ones like House Sparrow, Starling, Robin and Blackbird. Then some more unusual ones like Water Rail, Wryneck, Ostrich...'

'Ostrich!' cried Stickler.

'Damn good man, Edrich' muttered the Colonel from his corner at the bar, 'never afraid to give it a go. Remember the time when...' he mumbled on.

'Don't tell me what list it was' said Listman, 'I'm keen to guess. From what you just said it must be a world list of some kind.'

'Naturally' confirmed Twitchett, 'with Peregrine being such a traveller he was able to add to the list in a number of countries.

Peacock was another I can remember and of course the rarest was Stephen Island Wren.'

'Wait a minute, that last bird's extinct' interjected Listman. 'Only a handful were ever seen. It was killed off by the lighthouse keeper's cat.'

'Precisely' said Twitchett, smiling. 'It was a list of birds that the cat brought in.'

'But what about the Ostrich?' queried Stickler.

'That was when he was staying with his game warden friend in Kenya who had a pet lion' replied Twitchett. 'And the Peacock was caught by his friend the Maharaja's pet tiger.'

'Ridiculous' scoffed Stringwell. 'I think he just dreamed them all.'

'I know someone with a dream list...' began Stickler.

'I've had enough of lists' snapped Stringwell, who was clearly getting annoyed. 'Let's go back to talking about something sensible like what's going to turn up next.'

'Well the winds are supposed to be going round to north-east, which is usually a good sign' reported Listman. 'I think we're going to get a Sibe, and a few Pallas's Warblers if not something rarer.'

'Going back to dreams...' said Twitchett.

'I think I will' sniffed Stringwell and closed his eyes.

'I once knew someone whose wife had premonitions about birds turning up' continued Twitchett.

'And divorced her husband when she found out it was true?' suggested Stickler.

'If you're not going to take this seriously then I won't bother to continue' said Twitchett indignantly. He got up and walked over to the bar.

'Oh do come back' implored Listman. 'I'm listening, after all there's nothing else to do.'

Twitchett sulked for a few moments longer and then the impulse to go on with his tale grew too much for him and he returned to the table.

'This is a true story' he insisted. 'She used to dream about them and amazingly the dreams came true. Do you remember the Scarlet Tanager on St Mary's some years ago, well she dreamed about it a few days before it was found. Even pictured the area it was found in.'

'But anyone can say that after the event' said Stringwell, who had clearly been listening although pretending not to. 'Has anyone really put her to the test?'

'Well not that I know of' answered Twitchett. 'But it would be fun to try. I've got her husband's 'phone number in my notebook somewhere.' He pulled it from his pocket and flicked through. 'Yes, here it is.'

'Well go on then' they all said, 'give him a ring.'

Twitchett went to the 'phone at the bar and dialled the number. They could hear him talking and nodding his head. He jotted down a few things in his notebook, put the 'phone down and walked back to the table.

'Well, what did he say?' they all asked.

'He was understandably reluctant' said Twitchett. 'He didn't want his wife made fun of, but I explained that it was a sort of experiment and he agreed that he will ring as soon as she has another dream. All we can do is wait.'

The predicted north-easterly winds arrived and brought a small flurry of birds. An Isabelline Shrike in Suffolk, Olive-backed Pipit in Norfolk, three or four Pallas's Warblers and a scattering of Yellow-browed Warblers down the east coast.

A few days later the 'phone in the *Coot and Corncrake* rang for Twitchett. At last his friend's wife had been dreaming. Twitchett scribbled down some notes and returned to the table where his three friends waited eagerly.

'Well, not much to go on' he said, 'but let's see what we can make of it. She couldn't remember the details very clearly but got the impression that it was a dark grey bird and it had some red somewhere underneath or maybe on the head.'

'Red-footed Falcon' suggested Stickler. 'That's got red legs, red under the tail and a red eye-ring.'

'There's more to come' said Twitchett curtly. 'It wasn't a very large bird and it had a longish tail.'

'I still reckon it's the falcon' said Stickler. 'Size is relative after all. Was there any idea of where it was seen?'

'She said it was on the coast somewhere and there was a light-house nearby. She said it seemed familiar but she couldn't remember exactly where. There were bushes around, and grass, and a road ran right by it. There was a garden and the bird was either in a bush or on the ground.' They all sat thinking for a while.

'It couldn't be Dungeness if there are lots of bushes and grass but it might be Spurn' suggested Stringwell.

'It must be Portland Bill' announced Twitchett and the others all agreed this was the most likely place.

'Anything more about the bird?' asked Stringwell.

'Only that she didn't recognise it from any books afterwards' said Twitchett.

'How much in advance of the bird arriving are these dreams?' asked Stickler.

'Impossible to say but the bird is usually found two or three days afterwards' replied Twitchett.

They sat in silence for a few moments until Listman said 'Well, are we going to do it?'

'Do what?' asked Stringwell who was still puzzling about the identity of the bird.

'Test out the dream' replied Listman. 'Go to Portland and look for this bird, whatever it is.'

'Must be a Red-foot' insisted Stickler.

'I've thought of another alternative' said Stringwell. 'Small and grey with a long tail and some red around the eye and orangey legs... it could be a Marmora's Warbler. Portland would be a good place for it.'

'Like Sheffield was for the first one' sneered Stickler.

'Which you dipped on' jeered Stringwell.

The two of them glared at one another until Twitchett, who had just finished his pint, banged his glass down loudly and said 'Let's go tomorrow.' And so the decision was made.

They arrived at the Bill with light westerly winds blowing. Very few birds of note had been seen so far that day. A Reed Warbler had been potentially named as a dozen or so different rarities before it was eventually trapped in the observatory garden. A couple of Black Redstarts had been seen and there was a Firecrest by the quarry.

'Falcon flying right behind the observatory' cried Stickler, keen to prove his guess. A grey bird with pointed wings and a long tail flew across towards some bushes.

'Come off it Stickler' said Stringwell caustically, 'that's not even a bird of prey.'

Stickler shrugged and said 'Well at least I'm keeping my eyes open.'

They wandered around for an hour searching bushes and scanning the sky.

'Let's see what's on the sea' said Twitchett, trying to sound cheerful. But an hour of sitting by the Pyramid produced nothing more than a couple of Gannets, some Kittiwakes and a few indeterminate terns. Twitchett tried to string an Arctic Skua into a shearwater and justifiably misidentified a badly oiled adult Little Gull. The trip was turning out to be something of a disappointment, and the four birdwatchers were beginning to look decidedly bored. Listman started glancing furtively at his watch.

A return to the bushes brought one surge of excitement when Stringwell saw something small flit into a bush. They watched for ten minutes seeing only a vague movement within the vegetation.

'I can just make it out' said Stringwell excitedly. 'Grey underparts and reddish legs....' The bird hopped onto the ground and shuffled along, flicking its wings.

'Panic over' said Listman. 'Let's go to the pub.'

Things felt a little better after a couple of pints and a pasty and the four of them emerged refreshed and raring for rarities.

'Here comes a falcon' shouted Stickler, pointing excitedly to a distant silhouette flying towards them. The bird flew down to the edge of a field and began to hover.

'Must be a Kestrel' said Twitchett. 'Better luck next time.'

They walked down the road past the old lighthouse. Some noise of birds mobbing something attracted Twitchett's attention. A bird flew past him with three or four sparrows chasing it and chirruping. They disappeared behind a bush.

'Now, I wonder what that is?' muttered Twitchett, as he tip-toed over to investigate. A strange looking bird came out from behind the bush and Twitchett began to laugh.

'Over here' he called out to the others who quickly joined him. 'There it is' he said, laughing hysterically and pointing to a long-tailed dark-grey bird with red legs and a red eye-ring. It had white spotting on its back and didn't look happy.

'An escaped Diamond Dove' said Twitchett, wiping the tears from his eyes, 'no wonder she couldn't find it in a book.'

Released from their quest, the four decided to salvage some of the day by visiting Radipole, where they cheered themselves up with a Ring-billed Gull and a Red-rumped Swallow.

They got back to the *Coot and Corncrake* in time for a couple of drinks and Twitchett 'phoned for bird news. He returned to the table looking rather glum.

'She was right after all' he said. 'Grey with a long tail and reddish undertail coverts. Seen by a lighthouse and not in the books because the first one was only seen last year.'

'What on earth is it?' chorused the others.

'A Catbird, in a garden by the lighthouse on St Agnes. Anyone for Scillies?'

Questions: *1.* What erroneous statement did Twitchett make at Portland? *2.* What was the first 'falcon' that Stickler saw? *3.* What might Twitchett have called the Arctic Skua? *4.* What bird would Twitchett have identified the Little Gull as? *5.* What was the small bird Stringwell saw?

Four of a Feather

There are two parts to this quiz. The first 32 questions consist of a list of four birds, all of which have something in common. The second 32 questions also consist of four bird names but, in this case, one of them is an 'odd one out'.

What Have These Four in Common?

Q1. Surf Scoter, Long-billed Dowitcher, Lesser Yellowlegs, Pectoral Sandpiper.

Q2. Red-legged Partridge, Ruddy Duck, Egyptian Goose, Lady Amherst's Pheasant.

Q3. Grey Heron, Jay, Great Skua, Great Spotted Woodpecker.

Q4. Magpie, Buzzard, Chough, Dipper.

Q5. Swift, Puffin, Manx Shearwater, Storm Petrel.

Q6. Lapwing, Green Woodpecker, Dunnock, Bearded Tit.

Q7. Bermuda Petrel, White-winged Guan, Jerdan's Courser, Gurney's Pitta.

Q8. Owl-parrot, Kagu, Wren-thrush, Takahe.

Q9. Stock Dove, Redstart, Blue Tit, Kestrel.

Q10. Bee-eater, Shelduck, Puffin, Manx Shearwater.

Q11. Arctic Skua, Avocet, Eider, Arctic Tern.

Q12. Red Kite, House Martin, Black Tern, Greenfinch.

Q13. Kittiwake, Rook, Sand Martin, Black-headed Gull.

Q14. Pigeon, Warbler, Sandpiper, Duck.

Q15. Black-necked Grebe, Greenshank, Avocet, Red-throated Diver.

Q16. Dipper, Stone Curlew, Waxwing, Oystercatcher.

Q17. Wheatear, Kentish Plover, Great Grey Shrike, Bee-eater.

Q18. Red Kite, Carrion Crow, Great Black-backed Gull, Fulmar.

Q19. Firecrest, Redwing, Garganey, Sedge Warbler.

Q20. Whinchat, Willow Grouse, Corncrake, Brambling.

Q21. Goshawk, Oystercatcher, Bee-eater, Nuthatch.

Q22. Grasshopper Warbler, Chiffchaff, Whooper Swan, Nightjar.

Q23. Redpoll, Little Tern, Coot, Lesser Spotted Woodpecker.

Q24. Crane, Woodchat Shrike, Great Spotted Woodpecker, Linnet.

Q25. Mute Swan, Barnacle Goose, Common Gull, Marsh Tit.

Q26. Coal Tit, Goldcrest, Crossbill, Long-eared Owl.

Q27. Black-throated Diver, Green Woodpecker, Turnstone, Treecreeper.

Q28. Thrush Nightingale, Curlew Sandpiper, Hen Harrier, Hawk Owl.

Q29. Cuckoo, Tawny Owl, Arctic Skua, Fulmar.

Q30. Eider, Reed Warbler, Grasshopper Warbler, Reed Bunting.

Q31. Willow Tit, Wood Sandpiper, Marsh Harrier, Reed Bunting.

Q32. Little Crake, Golden Eagle, Pied Flycatcher, Common Sandpiper.

Which is the Odd One Out?

Q33. Reed Warbler, Great Reed Warbler, Bearded Reedling, Reed Bunting.

Q34. Wigeon, Teal, Pintail, Gadwall.

Q35. Ptarmigan, Greenshank, Snow Bunting, Dunlin.

Q36. Subalpine Warbler, Whitethroat, Lesser Whitethroat, Spectacled Warbler.

Q37. Black-billed Cuckoo, Eurasian Cuckoo, Great Spotted Curlew, Didric Cuckoo.

Q38. Common Gull, Glaucous Gull, Lesser Black-backed Gull, Slender-billed Gull.

Q39. Hen Harrier, Ruff, Great Crested Grebe, Bittern.

Q40. Buzzard, Honey Buzzard, Long-legged Buzzard, Rough-legged Buzzard.

Q41. Fieldfare, Black-headed Gull, Rook, Collared Dove.

Q42. Robin, Spotted Flycatcher, Wren, Blackbird.

Q43. Rock Partridge, Grey Partridge, Red-legged Partridge, Barbary Partridge.

Q44. Razorbill, Nightjar, Little Crake, Spotted Flycatcher.

Q45. Grey Heron, Crossbill, Tree Sparrow, Goldeneye.

Q46. Little Owl, Pheasant, Ring-necked Parakeet, White-tailed Eagle.

Q47. Sanderling, Chaffinch, Tufted Duck, Robin.

Q48. Black Duck, Black Kite, Black Grouse, Black Tern.

Q49. Chaffinch, Goldfinch, Linnet, Bullfinch.

Q50. Gannet, Shag, Red-throated Diver, Dabchick.

Q51. Starling, Lapwing, Mallard, Kittiwake.

Q52. Great Tit, Arctic Tern, Blackcap, House Martin.

Q53. Osprey, Stone Curlew, Waxwing, Oystercatcher.

Q54. Goldfinch, Jay, Kingfisher, Curlew Sandpiper.

Q55. Kingfisher, Long-tailed Tit, Yellow Wagtail, Bluethroat.

Q56. Great White Heron, Avocet, Sanderling, Pied Wagtail.

Q57. Great Skua, Great Black-backed Gull, Great Spotted Woodpecker, Great Grey Shrike.

Q58. Red-crested Pochard, Red-breasted Merganser, Red-legged Partridge, Red-breasted Flycatcher.

Q59. Black-headed Gull, Black-throated Diver, Black-eared Wheatear, Black-tailed Godwit.

Q60. Great Reed Warbler, Great Crested Grebe, Great Black-headed Gull, Great Snipe.

Q61. Spanish Sparrow, Snowfinch, White-throated Sparrow, Rock Sparrow.

Q62. Purple Heron, Golden Plover, White Stork, Yellow Wagtail.

Q63. Bearded Tit, Blue Tit,
Long-tailed Tit, Penduline Tit.

Q64. Hen Harrier, Golden
Eagle, Sparrowhawk, Merlin.

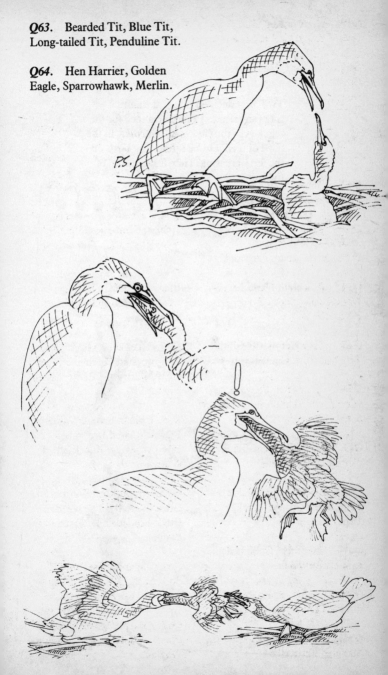

LEAVES FROM TWITCHETT'S NOTEBOOK

Twitchett decided to join the annual shopping trip to France arranged for the regulars of the *Coot and Corncrake*, in the hope of seeing some interesting birds on the ferry crossing. Here is his record of the trip.

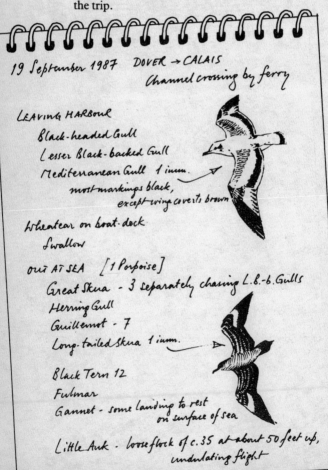

19 September 1987   DOVER → CALAIS
Channel crossing by ferry

LEAVING HARBOUR
Black-headed Gull
Lesser Black-backed Gull
Mediterranean Gull 1 imm.
    most markings black,
        except wing coverts brown

Wheatear on boat-deck
Swallow

OUT AT SEA   [1 Porpoise]
Great Skua - 3 separately chasing L.B.-b. Gulls
Herring Gull
Guillemot - 7
Long-tailed Skua 1 imm.

Black Tern 12
Fulmar
Gannet - some landing to rest
        on surface of sea

Little Auk - loose flock of c. 35 at about 50 feet up,
            undulating flight

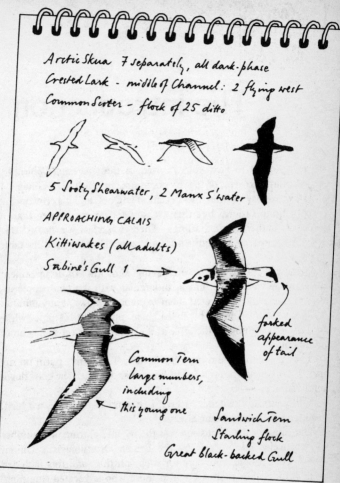

Arctic Skua 7 separately, all dark-phase
Crested Lark - middle of Channel: 2 flying west
Common Scoter - flock of 25 ditto

5 Sooty Shearwater, 2 Manx S'water

APPROACHING CALAIS

Kittiwakes (all adults)

Sabine's Gull 1 →

forked appearance of tail

Common Tern large numbers, including this young one ←

Sandwich Tern
Starling flock
Great black-backed Gull

Question: what are the five errors
Twitchett has made?

The Introduction

It was unusual to hear voices raised in the *Coot and Corncrake*, unless someone was trying to communicate with the Colonel – which was always a short-lived event. Twitchett and his crowd were usually quite orderly but this evening they were noisier than a pre-roost gathering of Starlings. There was clearly a heated discussion in progress and quite a crowd had gathered around the table to listen.

Stringwell and Listman were having some kind of disagreement and anyone watching who was unfamiliar with the two people involved might have expected them to come to blows at any minute. Twitchett was sitting in his usual chair, puffing at his pipe, while Stickler was leaning on the table as if about to interject some choice comment.

'I say it doesn't count' said Stringwell, 'I wouldn't put it on my list.' He downed what was left of his pint and banged the glass down on the table.

'Call yourself a twitcher,' jeered Listman. 'If you've seen a bird, it goes on the list. Nothing else matters.'

The cause of the discussion was the recent splitting of a number of subspecies into species by the British Ornithologist's Union. There were people who were for such splitting, and this included most birders, but there were also those who advocated 'lumping' and viewed with disapproval the rise to specific status of birds like the Scottish Crossbill. The most recent splitting had involved Rock and Water Pipits which had, overnight, been declared separate species thus providing, or so claimed Listman, an 'armchair tick'. The argument in progress was not between 'splitters' and 'lumpers' but was over when you could count these additions to your list.

'Yes, but you can't count it in retrospect' insisted Stringwell. 'You've got to see it after the announcement from the BOU has been made. What about that Sora on Scilly in 1973? It was identified at first as a Spotted Crake and not correctly pinned down until many people, including you, had left. You didn't tick that off later.'

'That's totally different – if you don't identify the bird when you see it then of course you can't tick it' retorted Listman.

'I seem to remember' interrupted Twitchett, 'that a certain Least Sandpiper on your list was only identified by virtue of its gammy leg.'

'Ah, well y-yes', stammered Listman 'but it had been watched by everyone else there at closer quarters, I mean it clearly was the Least Sand, they had all watched it fly over to that island before I arrived and anyway I had to dash off after…'

'Who's for another drink' said Twitchett who delighted in winding up Listman when he got onto this subject.

Stickler, who had been sitting quietly not getting involved, suddenly took the opportunity to join in the discussion.

'What about introductions?' he asked.

'Don't be silly you know us all' said Listman, not really concentrating on what Stickler had said.

'Do you mean the sort of introductions that Twitchett's great grand-father made – the 'Halstead Rarities'?' enquired Stringwell smiling in Twitchett's direction. Twitchett scowled at him and banged his pipe noisily in the ashtray..

'No' said Stickler. 'I mean what if you saw a Ruddy Duck before it was put on the list?'

'Count it!' said Listman. 'No doubt about it.'

'Rubbish' cried Stringwell, his voice beginning to move up an octave. 'If it wasn't breeding in sufficient numbers to qualify when you saw it, it doesn't count.'

The pair of them again began to shout at one another with such force that the Colonel started applauding. 'Well done' he shouted. 'You can't beat a bit of English willow. Let's have a follow on.' Rossie quietened him down with a gin and tonic.

'I don't think they should be on the list at all' said Twitchett, returning with a round of drinks. 'Nothing but a load of foreign pheasants and delinquent ducks!' He sat back in his chair with a faint smile on his face, extracted a pipe cleaner from his top pocket and picked up his pipe.

'But if you don't count introductions that means that Little Owl wouldn't count' said Listman.

'Nor Capercaillie' interjected Stickler.

'Precisely' said Twitchett. 'They're just not British.'

This provoked a further furious debate with Listman claiming that any of the small Canada Goose races which sometimes occur must be genuine and that it was quite conceivable that a Little Owl could cross the Channel. Stringwell was so overexcited that he drank half of Stickler's lager without realising it.

Twitchett sat through all of this with a curious half-smile on his face. As they began to quieten down he refilled his pipe, sat back in his chair and said loudly 'That reminds me of a story which would interest you, Listman.' The table went quiet and all eyes were on Twitchett.

'It concerned a twitcher who one or two of you may remember, Chas King. He was quite a big lister in his day – went for absolutely anything. He once went for an Ovenbird on Shetland, a Sharp-tailed Sandpiper in Wales and a Yellow-rumped Warbler on the Scillies in the space of a few days. Whenever he saw a new bird you would think he had won the pools.

'He also had a reputation for letting nothing come between him and a bird. One autumn, he had spent the last couple of weeks of September on Fair Isle, where he had seen Citrine Wagtail, Red-throated Pipit and Pechora Pipit. He then went to Scilly, where he saw Tawny and Richard's Pipits. There was only one left, at that time, for him to have seen all of the wagtails and pipits within a month, as he had also seen all of the common ones during this period. Two days before the month was up an Olive-backed Pipit was found on Tresco in the late afternoon. Chas was one of the last people to get there before dark and the small group of birders watching the bird told him that it had just walked into some short grass in front of them and was out of sight for the moment. He stood there for about three minutes physically twitching with antici-pation and then suddenly, with a cry of 'I'm going in' he started forward into the grass. Not believing their ears and eyes the group of birders nearly let him get away with it, but one of them grabbed and forcibly held him until the bird walked out into the open of its own accord. And that wasn't the only occasion when he had to be physically restrained and gagged to prevent him scaring the bird away.

'Apart from the size of his list, his biggest boast was that it contained no introduced birds. He actually didn't count Little Owl or Capercaillie and he never had or would look for Lady Amherst's or Golden Pheasants or any other foreign exotics. Such was his contempt when the BOU admitted Ring-necked Parakeet onto the list that we all thought he was going to emigrate. I believe he even wrote to his MP to complain. Anyway it was his vociferous dislike for these birds and his pompous attitude about his list that became his downfall.' Twitchett paused to drain his pint and waited until it had been refilled before continuing.

'It was spring 1984 and a Collared Flycatcher had been seen at a park in Margate. You dipped on that one, didn't you Listman?'

'Just a partial albino Pied Fly if you ask me' mumbled Listman, who had been five times to look for the bird without any success at all. He started to go rather pink in the face.

'Chas was there immediately' continued Twitchett. 'A car full of us had driven with him overnight and we were there at dawn. There were about two hundred people there, spread out in the park. The bird was very elusive, appearing before a few people for a couple of seconds and then disappearing for half an hour. It was three hours before the bird appeared in front of us, flitting between the tops of the trees. A beautiful male.' Listman groaned and went to get another round in. 'As usual, Chas had no real sense of occasion. He jumped up and down, danced around, cheered and kept shouting "One more" at the top of his voice. He only quietened down when a rather burly birder from Liverpool threatened to show him a new place to keep his telescope.

'One of the chaps in our car, Bob, came from Kent originally and was chatting to some of the local birders there. They told him that a Golden Oriole had been seen and heard the previous day in west Kent. If we wanted to take a look on the way back, he knew where it was. We decided to pop in to Stodmarsh first to try and get Savi's Warbler for the year. We parked in the car park and began to walk along the bank. There were Cetti's Warblers singing, Bearded Tits calling and bobbing over the reeds. A Marsh Harrier flew across the reedbed and put up a Bittern, a couple of Garganey flew over and then, in the distance, we heard a rattling trill. It sounded slower than a Grasshopper Warbler and was clearly a Savi's. Bob eventually spotted it sitting in a bush but Chas couldn't locate it. In typical fashion, he pushed Bob out of the way to get a look at it.

"What's next?" shouted Chas. "Our luck's with us today. Let's go on somewhere else before it runs out."

' "I wish he'd run out." Bob muttered. "Into the marsh – it will take ten feet of mud to keep him quiet."

'As we had plenty of time we also stopped at Cliffe Marshes to look for a White-rumped Sandpiper that had been seen there earlier in the week. There was a good wader flock on show with a nice summer plumaged Little Stint, a couple of Temminck's Stints, a Purple Sandpiper, Bar-tailed and Black-tailed godwits and several hundred Dunlin. Finally we saw the White-rumped Sand fly in, easily recognisable with its white rump and white wing stripe as it landed amongst the Dunlin. Once again, Chas was beside himself and we all thought Bob was going to explode when he started clapping his hands with excitement and flushed the flock of waders, which flew to an inaccessible corner of the marshes.

'So we decided that we should go for the oriole next and then head for home. We arrived at the spot, which was a small piece of woodland with adjacent orchards. The bird, Bob explained, had been heard in the wood and seen in the orchard. We split up and began to search. After about fifteen minutes, we heard a shout from Bob and hurried towards where he stood by his 'scope pointing. Chas was the first to reach him and we all saw him look through the 'scope and then jump back with a loud scream of rage. "You lousy bunch of .....s" he cried, his face turning red and with what looked like tears in his eyes. He pushed over Bob's tripod and 'scope, which luckily landed on grass, ran off down the road and I've never seen him since. The last I heard of him he had virtually stopped birding in this country and was leading bird tours abroad.'

Twitchett stopped and began to clean and replenish his pipe.

'But what had happened?' asked the others in unison.

'Well it was a nasty trick' answered Twitchett. 'Bob had always been a practical joker and the place he took us to was not the Golden Oriole spot at all. He had actually taken us to somewhere he knew only too well, and what Chas saw when he looked down the 'scope was a hole in a tree with a Ring-necked Parakeet sitting next to it. It wasn't just the fact that he had seen one that really caused the trouble. The "one more" he had shouted earlier meant that he only needed one to get his 400th bird.'

Quetions: *1.* Which bird was not likely to have been seen? *2.* Which bird did they misidentify at Stodmarsh and why? *3.* Which bird did they definitely misidentify at Cliffe and what was it really? *4.* Why might you not count Capercaillie on your list.

General Knowledge

Q1. What is *Troglodytes troglodytes*?

Q2. What is *Cettia cetti*?

Q3. What passerine has been recorded the furthest north?

Q4. What birds have been recorded the furthest south?

Q5. What bird on the British list is also known as a Zitting Cisticola?

Q6. What British wader habitually bobs its tail?

Q7. What two waders breed the furthest south in Britain?

Q8. What finch breeds the furthest north in Britain?

Q9. What is *Pica pica*?

Q10. What is *Picus viridis*?

Q11. What habitat do Bitterns breed in?

Q12. What habitat do Ring Ousels breed in?

Q13. How do Little Grebes differ from other grebes in flight?

Q14. What wader has a towering flight and trilling call when disturbed?

Q15. Name three hirundines which breed in Britain.

Q16. Name four auks which breed in Britain.

Q17. What is *Mergus serrator* ?

Q18. What is *Sterna sandvicensis*?

Q19. What marine duck forms creches?

Q20. What duck is named after the shape of its bill?

Q21. What lark is an uncommon winter visitor and rare breeder in Britain?

Q22. What bunting is an uncommon winter visitor and a recent rare breeder in Britain?

Q23. Which is the most northerly breeding thrush in Britain?

Q24. Which is the most northerly breeding warbler in Britain?

Q25. What is *Locustella naevia*?

Q26. What is *Regulus ignicapillus*?

Q27. Where do British Swallows spend the winter?

Q28. Where do British Sand Martins spend the winter?

Q29. Why do woodpeckers drum?

Q30. Why do fulmars regurgitate oil?

Q31. Which tree does the Jay help to disperse?

Q32. How does a shrike store its food?

Q33. What is *Nucifraga caryocatactes*?

Q34. What is *Pernis apivorus*?

Q35. Where is Humberside's bird observatory?

Q36. Where is Dorset's bird observatory?

Q37. What is a mist net?

Q38. What prominent feature do Black-necked and Slavonian Grebes show in breeding plumage?

Q39. What prominent feature do Knot and Curlew Sandpiper show in breeding plumage?

Q40. What is a Heligoland trap?

Q41. Why might a Ringed Plover pretend to have a broken wing?

Q42. Why might a male Chaffinch attack a car hub-cap?

Q43. What is *Fulmarus glacialis*?

Q44. What is *Columba palumbus*?

Q45. How many toes does a Ringed Plover have?

Q46. How many toes does a Swift have?

Q47. How many eggs does a Gannet lay?

Q48. How many eggs does a Cormorant lay?

Q49. Where do Swallows roost away from the nest?

Q50. Where do Swifts roost away from the nest?

Q51. What is *Ardea purpurea*?

Q52. What is *Streptopelia turtur*?

Q53. What is the main food of the Capercaillie in winter?

Q54. How do gulls open shells?

Q55. Are birds left- and right-footed?

Q56. Are birds colour-blind?

Q57. Why does a phalarope spin on water?

Q58. Why can't a Treecreeper climb down a tree trunk?

Q59. Do skylarks only sing when flying?

Q60. Could you hear a Mute Swan?

Q61. What is *Anas platyrhynchos*?

Q62. What is *Turdus merula*?

Q63. The name of what British winter visitor contains all the vowels once only?

Q64. The name of what common and widespread British breeding bird contains all the vowels once only?

The
Three Feathers

Twitchett was in a furious temper. He was thumping his fist on the table with such force that ashtrays, glasses, and cigarette lighters were performing little quadrilles on the surface, and a considerable amount of beer was slopping about.

Even Rossie, our normally tolerant landlord, was driven to remonstrate. 'Now look, Twitchett, calm down, can't you. I'll lose my licence if you keep this racket up.'

But Twitchett couldn't even hear him above the sound of his own voice. '... evil, unprincipled vulture-faced pig' he roared '... that unadulterated, undiluted heap of foetid bird droppings... if he thinks he can get away with this, he had better think again. I'll sue him from here to eternity... I'll... '. Evidently he could think of no threat or curse foul enough for the occasion. In sheer frustration he let out a bellow of rage 'Yaaaaargh' and bought his fist down again with such a crash that Listman leapt out of his seat and retreated nervously towards the bar, while Stickler looked for a moment as though he were going to take refuge under the table, until, just in time he realised that this might well be the worst possible place to be. They had seen Twitchett in a temper before, but this bore as much relationship to one of his ordinary tantrums as did a tsunami to a ripple on a duck pond.

For the time being, however, he seemed to have exhausted himself. He sat in his chair, snorting and glowering, like a bull who has just seen a juicy matador hopping over to the other side of the fence. He seemed to be oblivious to what was going on around him.

'Had we better get a straight jacket?' asked Listman dubiously.

'Or an undertaker?' suggested Listman in a misjudged attempt at flippancy.

'What's the matter with him anyway?' asked Stickler. 'I've never seen him like this before – except, perhaps, for the time when his record of a Demoiselle Crane was rejected.'

'It's the heat' said the Colonel judiciously. 'Seen it all before. Can't take it. Not wearing a hat, you see.' Since it had been a heavily overcast day, with chilly March winds, nobody seemed inclined to take this suggestion seriously.

'I think' said Rossie, 'that it may have something to do with that letter he's got in his hand. I suggest that we take a look at it. Meanwhile, I think Twitchett could probably do with a stiff drink.'

He poured several measures of Famous Grouse into a glass and took it over to Twitchett's chair. 'Here you are', he said 'on the house', and deftly manoeuvred the glass into Twitchett's hand, while simultaneously relieving him of the mysterious letter. 'Right', he said. 'Let's see what all this is about.'

At first sight, the letter seemed innocuous enough. It was from Algernon Gripsall – not one of Twitchett's greatest friends, admittedly – but the tone was polite enough, and there didn't seem to be anything in it that could have caused offence on the cataclysmic scale they had just witnessed. 'Dear Twitchett' it read. 'I hope you will forgive this intrusion on your time, but I am hoping that you will be able to give me some information. I am currently editing the wartime memoirs of my great uncle Torquemada Gripsall with a view to publication. As you may know, my great uncle was a childhood companion of your own great uncle Tarquin Twitchett, and both saw action in the trenches during the First World War. There are several interesting references to him in the diaries. I wondered therefore if you, or any member of your family, might still have any of your great uncle's own diaries, or correspondence, since these might well help in filling out the record. I would be most grateful for any assistance you might be able to give. Yours etc. Algernon Gripsall.'

'It's almost suspiciously polite' said Listman. 'They never normally even speak to each other. Do you think it's a forgery?'

'I doubt it' said Stringwell. 'Look, its got dirty finger marks on it – it must be Gripsall's work. I think Twitchett is just being jolly silly.'

'So you think that, do you?' came a voice from behind them. 'Well, I can tell you that there is vicious dirty work afoot.' It was Twitchett, apparently somewhat calmed down by the generous helping of Famous Grouse. The glass was now empty in front of him. 'I can tell you what that foul-minded slanderer is intending to do; he is going to resurrect that awful story of my great uncle Tarquin. And not only does it affect the honour of every Twitchett, it is *completely untrue*.'

Listman, Stringwell and Stickler looked at each other with some surprise. They were taken aback by the thought that Twitchett had a story about his uncle Tarquin and they had never heard it, however awful it might be. Such considerations had never been known to affect Twitchett's storytelling before. 'What awful story?' asked Listman.

For once in his life, Twitchett seemed almost reluctant to take the centre of the stage. 'I probably haven't told you the tale of my great uncle Tarquin' he said. 'It is rather tragic. Still, I suppose you had better hear it now.'

'It all began in the early years of the century. As you all know, by now, there was never any love lost between the Gripsalls and the Twitchetts, but my great uncle Tarquin's family had, by ill-chance, found themselves living in a rural part of the county where their nearest neighbours were members of the Gripsall clan. The adults of course refused to speak to each other, but young Tarquin was probably too young to appreciate the true nature of these fiends. Anyway, as both he and young Torquemada were birwatchers from the cradle (my great uncle's cradle list reached 72 before he moved to a larger bed), it was fairly natural that they should fall in with each other. I believe that my great uncle once swapped one of his precious Pallas's Sand Grouse eggs for two of Torquemada's Golden Orioles and a White-tailed Eagle; it wasn't until years later that he discoved that both the Golden Orioles were fakes.

'Of the two, there was no doubt that it was Tarquin who was the better birder. He was particularly expert on plumages, and built up a huge collection of birds' feathers. My great grandfather used to lock all the pillows away in the silver cupboard when Tarquin came to stay, for fear that he would tear them to pieces in search of a new specimen. Once, when he forgot, Tarquin claimed to have found two Spectacled Eider feathers in a consignment of my great grandmother's Harrods de luxe 'Regals' although he had to dismantle thirty of them in the process and it took the maid six months to clear up the mess.

'Anyway, a certain jealous rivalry had arisen between Tarquin and Torquemada by the time war broke out in 1914, and relationships were beginning to turn sour. At this stage, Torquemada found that he had joined the army. He hadn't, in fact, intended to enlist – his life list was only one behind Tarquin's, and he fully expected to overtake in the near future. However, as is usually the case with Gripsalls, greed got the better of him. He was discovered while attempting to sign up at every recruiting post in the area in the hope of getting a shilling from each one, and was promptly shipped off to France. Tarquin, in the meantime had volunteered in the usual way, but had been rejected on medical grounds – apparently, all those hours of digging around inside feather pillows had given him some rare and debilitating lung disease.

'Torquemada, of course, would never believe that my great uncle had tried to enlist. The thought of Tarquin roving about, adding all manner of rarities to his list, while he shivered in the trenches, must have driven him half round the bend. Eventually, it all got too much for him. He sent Tarquin an envelope from the front. Inside it were three feathers. They weren't exactly white feathers – in fact they ranged from blue to brown – but presumably feathers were rather hard to come by in the trenches, so he had to make do with what he could get. In any case, the message was clear. He was calling my great uncle a coward.

'Whether or not Tarquin was stung by Torquemada's message, I don't know. He was certainly in uniform and on the boat to France – carrying a forged medical certificate – within a matter of days, but this had nothing to do with the accusation of cowardice. Ironically, it had everything to do with the feathers. You see, Tarquin was sure that one of the feathers in the envelope belonged to a bird that he and his father had tried to see on a boyhood holiday to Cornwall: a Belted Kingfisher. Furthermore, one of the other feathers looked suspiciously as though it might belong to an immature of the same species. If there was a Belted Kingfisher breeding somewhere in northern France, Tarquin had to find it.

'His first few months at the front depressed him profoundly. His letters home recorded the dreariness of the trenches; the lack of any interesting birdlife. He bemoans the absence of birdsong. His requests for birdwatching leave were consistently refused. His notebooks for the period seem to contain little other than observations of the preening behaviour of Crested Larks. A few interesting things turned up: Hoopoe, Sardinian Warbler, Serin, Crested Tit and Icterine Warbler, for example; but they were few and far between. Certainly, of Belted Kingfishers there was no sign, and it was in an attempt to get closer to an area where they might be found that he eventually managed to get himself transferred. Gripsall's letter had come from somewhere on the Somme, and it was as part of an artillery regiment, being moved up to the Somme in preparation for a big offensive, that Tarquin found himself in something like a suitable habitat for a kingfisher. His last letter from the front is much more cheerful than its predecessors. He seemed to think that he might, at last, see something that would make the whole effort worthwhile.'

Here Twitchett paused. He seemed to be lost in his private thoughts. 'Poor fellow. Poor fellow' he muttered. 'What a dilemma. And what courage. One of the true heroes of our times.' He took another pull at his glass of whisky, and, with a visible effort, dragged himself back to his narrative.

The next thing anybody heard was a telegram from the War

Office. They announced that Tarquin was missing, presumed captured by the enemy, and that, in his absence, he had been tried for desertion or cowardice or some such rot, found guilty, and condemned to death. My great-great grandfather was devastated, of course. No Twitchett had ever been guilty of cowardice, let alone desertion, through centuries of valiant service to their country. He knew a mistake had been made. But the facts looked black.

'It appears that Tarquin had arrived on the battlefield at a crucial moment. The British armies were in the process of launching the eagerly awaited major offensive, which, it was fully expected, would effectively mark the end of the war. The offensive failed, and the Germans promptly counter-attacked. In the chaos of the battlefield, there seemed little to stop them. The whole story of that day's fighting has been told on innumerable occasions in histories of the war; it was the occasion on which we came nearest to losing the whole shooting match. A small unit of German troops broke through the front line of British defences, and once the dam was burst, the danger of total collapse was only too evident. All that stood between the advancing Germans and victory was Tarquin's small unit of artillery, quickly brought up in the rear, and armed with a motley collection of cannon of unknown provenance.

'The field was clear: the Germans were advancing in full view across level fields towards a small tributary of the Somme. The guns, with Tarquin in command, were well placed on the opposite bank to control the crossing, and could have wreaked havoc among the unfortunate German troops. The only thing missing was the command to fire, and the person supposed to be giving it was my great uncle Tarquin. The gun crews waited expectantly, but the command never came. When one of the corporals attempted, at the last moment, to fire the largest of the cannon he was, according to the court martial transcript, told to "leave that thing alone. If you fire that, I'll knock your block off."

'In the hand-to-hand fighting that followed, Tarqin acquitted himself valiantly. But it was hopeless. They were overpowered, and the survivors taken prisoner. Tarquin spent the rest of the war behind barbed wire in a damp bit of Silesia.

'If the Germans had pushed home their advantage, the war might have been lost that day. But they didn't. It turned out that the German High Command were neither expecting a break-through just then, nor, when it came, did they know what to do with it. Furthermore, they had made themselves thoroughly comfortable in a commandeered chateau behind the lines, and were loth to move. So they ordered their troops back again.

'Tarquin was lucky to have been captured that day. Had he

survived, the British Army would undoubtedly have had him shot. As it was, he never returned to England. He spent his time in Silesia trying to capture migrating Pintail, Pochard, Garganey, Gadwall or Teal, so that he could hide messages – about troop movements and so forth – inside rings on their legs. None of them ever reached any known destination, probably because he never did have a very good sense of direction and must have ringed them while they were going the wrong way. However, he did become friendly with the camp commandant, a Prussian aristocrat with a keen interest in birds himself. After the war, the commandant offered him the job of warden on a huge estate in the Pripet Marshes, and he took it. The family only ever received one more letter from him, some years after the end of the war. It was this that explained the whole incident, and revealed my great uncle to have been anything other than a coward. In fact, in my view, he should have been awarded a medal. Certainly he deserves the thanks and applause of all right thinking people. To those who know the truth, Tarquin's conduct showed great nobility and courage, and the accusations of cowardice are revealed as mere fabrications, a tissue of lies.

'War' mused Twitchett 'is debasing to the human spirit. Civilised values go by the board. Men's worst atavistic instincts are allowed full play. That is why any individual who demonstrates a concern for higher values shines like a beacon in the dreary landscape of battle. Tarqin was one such man. His actions that day must rank among the great heroic deeds of battle. I like to think that he was eventually welcomed, with open arms, into Valhalla – or wherever noble warriors get sent from far flung bits of Prussia. He deserves his reward. He would never have got it on earth – not while there were Gripsalls around to hound him.'

'Doesn't sound too heroic to me' commented Stringwell, clearly getting a bit impatient with Twitchett's reflections on the philosophy of war. 'Nearly loses us the war, and then expects a medal for it. Come on Twitchett. We all know about the incredible bravery of your ancestors, but it sounds as though this one laid an egg.'

'Sounds as though he was a bit loopy, to me' opined Stickler. 'Belted Kingfishers in the trenches of Northern France! Pshaw!!'

'Ah, but that's where you're wrong' said Twitchett. Tarquin found the Belted Kingfishers: *and* they were nesting at the time. That was what caused his dilemma and forced him to make one of the cruellest decisions a man can be called on to make. In the end, he found himself unable to give the order to fire those cannon at the crucial time. He chose life rather than slaughter. The nest was inside the barrel of the gun.'

His listeners looked stunned by this revelation. Listman was the first to speak again. 'Good Lord' he said. 'Now I understand. Poor Tarquin. I wish I had met him. I would like to have shaken his hand.'

'A unique breeding record for Europe' said Stickler, wistfully. 'I suppose the brood did survive?'

'No, alas' said Twitchett. They were blasted out of the barrel during the next big push – or perhaps the one after that. And so Tarquin's noble sacrifice was in vain.'

'Still, I see what you mean about heroism' said Stringwell. 'I think we ought to observe a minute's silence in his memory, and drink a toast to him.'

'I agree' said Listman.

'Very well' said Twitchett. He raised his glass solemnly. 'Gentlemen. I give you the memory of Tarquin Twitchett.'

'Tarquin Twitchett' they repeated respectfully, as they raised their glasses to their lips.

Questions: *1.* Why would Twitchett's Demoiselle Crane have been rejected? *2.* Which of Tarquin's wartime observations was likely to have been incorrect? *3.* Which duck would Tarquin have wasted his time trying to catch, and why?

P.S.

115

Answers

Page 17

1. Woodpigeons. *2.* Twitchett is more likely to have seen a Black-eared Wheatear, which has a very similar tail pattern to the Pied. *3.* Jack Snipe: they are normally silent, and Gropper would not have heard one without seeing it.

Pages 18-20

1. Moorhens and House Martins. *2.* Long-tailed Tits. *3.* Pigeons and Doves. *4.* 1,500 insects. *5.* Six days. *6.* Carrion Crow. *7.* Twenty-one. *8.* Fourteen. *9.* House Sparrow. *10.* Starling. *11.* Six. *12.* Three. *13.* Herring Gull and Kingfisher. *14.* Mistle Thrush and Hawfinch. *15.* Ibis. *16.* Falcon. *17.* Hummingbird. *18.* To moult. *19.* Twite. *20.* Greenland. It is a separate race of Wheatear. *21.* A sharp tip to the bill of a hatching bird which enables it to crack open the egg-shell. *22.* It is cracked and starting to hatch. *23.* Turnstone. *24.* House Sparrow. *25.* Red-legged Partridge. *26.* British Ornithologist's Union. *27.* Grebes. *28.* Woodcock. *29.* Skylark. *30.* It has no black collar. *31.* Whooper Swan. *32.* Manx Shearwater. *33.* A small *Calidris* wader, particularly an American stint, for example a Semi-palmated Sandpiper. *34.* A quieter song than the main territorial song, often uttered by immature birds in the autumn. *35.* The ability to mimic speech, as shown, for example, by parrots and mynahs. *36.* A Great Auk. *37.* Seventeen (including Shelduck). *38.* Eleven. *39.* Cuckoo. *40.* Hoopoe. *41.* Starlings. *42.* Pigeons. *43.* Collared Dove. *44.* Wryneck. *45.* Green Woodpecker. *46.* Winter, when it is mottled white and black. *47.* It has red waxy tips to its secondaries. *48.* Canada Goose. *49.* Brent Goose. *50.* They are lobed rather than webbed. *51.* Black Grouse and Ruffs. *52.* Red-breasted Goose. (55 cm., 1,000 gm.) *53.* Canada Goose. (95 cm., 5,000 gm.) *54.* By the unique black and yellow patterns on their bills. *55.* Rabbits. *56.* After St Peter, who walked on water. *57.* Golden Eagle. *58.* Ringed (largest), Kentish, Little Ringed. *59.* Continental Europe and Iceland. *60.* Because of its red forehead or 'poll'. *61.* Because 'dun' means brown; '-nock' is a diminutive, hence, literally, 'little brown job'. *62.* Water Rail. *63.* Pheasant. *64.* Immature Mistle Thrushes are spotted and streaked with buff-white above.

Page 25

Twitchett's six errors are as follows: *1.* The drawing shows a male not a female Hen Harrier. *2.* There are no Twite breeding in Wales. *3.* There are no Corn Bunting breeding in upland Wales. *4.* Red-breasted Merganser doesn't breed at Lake Vyrnwy; the drawing shows a female Goosander. *5.* There are no Red Kites at Lake Vyrnwy: the drawing is of a Buzzard. *6.* There are no Nightingales breeding in Central Wales.

Pages 26-28

1. Black. *2.* Red-pink. *3.* Pink. *4.* Red. *5.* Blue. *6.* Red with yellow tip. *7.* Yellow with black tip. *8.* White. *9.* Grey. *10.* White. *11.* Grey. *12.* Black. *13.* Red-pink. *14.* Black and white. *15.* Grey-brown. *16.* Black. *17.* Yellow. *18.* Brown-black. *19.* White shading to brown below. *20.* White. *21.* White. *22.* Blue-grey with black terminal band. *23.* White. *24.* Orange-buff. *25.* Black. *26.* Grey. *27.* Dark grey. *28.* White. *29.* Grey-black. *30.* Black with yellow tip. *31.* Brown. *32.* Orange-red. *33.* Bluish-white. *34.* Yellow-orange. *35.* Red. *36.* Yellow-green. *37.* Black. *38.* Yellow. *39.* Yellow. *40.* Rufous. *41.* White. *42.* Black. *43.* Black. *44.* Pale brown. *45.* Black. *46.* White. *47.* Black. *48.* Orange. *49.* Yellow. *50.* Grey brown. *51.* Brown-black. *52.* Dark brown. *53.* Yellow-brown. *54.* Slate blue. *55.* Black. *56.* Pale brown. *57.* Yellow-brown. *58.* Orange-red with yellow tip. *59.* Grey-black. *60.* Yellow. *61.* Brown. *62.* Pale grey. *63.* Grey. *64.* Black.

Page 35

1. Labrador Ducks are extinct. *2*. Red-tailed Tropicbirds do not occur off the West African coast. *3*. Arctic Warblers breed in northern Europe but migrate to south-east Asia for the winter.

Pages 36-39

1. The male starling has a blue base to its bill, the female a pink one. *2*. Male ruffs are larger. *3*. Willow warblers have pale legs, Chiffchaffs have dark legs. *4*. The Rook has long, shaggy feathers which cover the upper leg, the Carrion Crow doesn't. *5*. The Marsh Tit has a glossy black crown, the Willow Tit has a dull sooty black crown. *6*. Pied Wagtails have a black back in summer and a black rump at all times, White Wagtails have a pale grey back and a grey rump at all times. *7*. Young Swallows do not have long tail streamers. *8*. Young Goldcrests lack the black and yellow crown patch of the adults. *9*. Both male and female House martins incubate, only the female Swallow does. *10*. Oystercatchers in winter have a white half collar on their throat. *11*. The Scandinavian race has a red spot, the central European race has a white spot. *12*. West European Lesser Black-backed Gulls have a slate-grey back, Scandinavian birds have a darker slate-black back. *13*. The British Dipper has a chestnut belly, the Continental race has a black belly. *14*. British Long-tailed Tits have black crown stripes, N European birds have an all-white head. *15*. Male Mute Swans have a large black knob at the base of the bill. *16*. The male Nightjar has a white patch on each wing-tip and white patches on either side of the tip of its tail. *17*. Long-eared Owls usually nest in old crow's nests, Short-eared owls only nest on the ground. *18*. Spotted Flycatchers nest in open nests on ledges or in creepers and walls, Pied Flycatchers nest in holes and trees and enclosed nest-boxes. *19*. Crossbills mainly feed on spruce seeds, Scottish Crossbills prefer pine seeds. *20*. The Greenland race of the Brent Goose has a pale belly while the Russian race has a dark belly. *21*. Adult Peregrines have barred underparts, juveniles are streaked. *22*. Whinchats have white outer-tail feathers, Stonechats don't. *23*. Juvenile Ring-necked Parakeets lack the neck-ring and resemble females, but have a horn coloured, rather than red bill. *24.* Juveniles do not have a white face and lack the black-barred belly of the adult. *25.* Whitethroats have a dancing song-flight, Lesser Whitethroats simply sing from bushes. *26.* Red-throated Divers moult in the autumn, the other divers moult just before the breeding season. *27.* The bill of a Black-necked Grebe is thinner and uptilted. *28.* A Great Crested Grebe's bill is pinkish, a Red-necked Grebe's bill is shorter and black with a yellow base. *29.* Buntings have stout bills for eating seeds, warblers have fine bills for eating insects. *30.* The Whooper Swan has a black bill with a large, pointed yellow patch on the sides. The Bewick's Swan has a black bill with a smaller, rounded yellow patch. *31.* A female Scaup has a white face, a female Tufted Duck has little or no white around the bill and may show a little head tuft. *32.* Drake Tufted Ducks have a black head glossed with purple, Scaup have a black head glossed with green. *33.* Velvet Scoters have white secondaries which form a white wing-panel in flight. *34.* Ringed Plovers have a white wing bar, Little Ringed Plovers have an all-brown wing. *35.* A supercilium is immediately above the eye, an eye-stripe is through the eye. *36.* An orbital ring is the bare skin around the eye, an eye-ring is formed by contrasting coloured feathers around the eye. *37.* Both have black crowns but the Little Tern has a white forehead which extends above the eye. *38.* Both have black heads but the Mediterranean Gull has white crescents above and below the eye. *39.* Bearded Tits eat mainly insects in the summer and reed seeds in the winter. *40.* Eiders feed mainly on molluscs such as mussels, Cormorants feed on fish. *41.* Mallard dabble and up-end for their food, Tufted Ducks dive underwater. *42.* Sparrowhawks chase their prey, often flying low along hedges. Kestrels spot their prey from a perch or when hovering and drop on it. *43.* The Nuthatch has three forward toes and one hind toe on each foot, Great Spotted Woodpeckers have two forward toes and two hind toes on each foot. *44.* Great Northern Divers have their three front toes webbed, Shags have all four toes webbed. *45.* Juvenile Kittiwakes have a black band at the end of the tail, adults have an all-white tail. *46.* None. *47.* Redshanks call 'tuu-hu-hu', Greenshanks have a lower 'tew, tew, tew' call. *48.* Chaffinches call 'chink', Bramblings call a hoarse 'tsweek'. *49.* Little Gulls have a black underwing, Mediterranean Gulls have a white underwing. *50.* The Collared Pratincole has a chestnut underwing, the Black-winged Pratincole has a black underwing. *51.* Guillemots have a more rounded and shorter tail, Razorbills are longer and more pointed. *52.* Reed Warblers have a rounded tail, Icterine warblers have a square-ended tail. *53.* The bill of a male Bearded Tit is yellow, a female's is brown. *54.* The bill of a female Goldeneye has a yellow tip. *55.* Both feed largely on insect larvae but the Great Spotted Woodpecker eats nuts and seeds, while the Green Woodpecker eats ants. **56.** Little Terns feed on fish, Black Terns feed on insects. **57.** The bill of a Bar-tailed Godwit is slightly upturned, that of a Black-tailed Godwit is straight. **58.** Little Ringed Plovers have a black bill, Ringed Plovers have an orange bill with a black tip. **59.** Sparrowhawks have rounded wing-tips, Kestrels have pointed wing-tips. **60.** None. **61.** The male is larger. **62.** The female is larger. **63.** Rock Pipits nest in rock crevices, Tree Pipits nest in tussocks on the ground. **64.** Reed Warblers nest off the ground in reeds, Reed Buntings nest on the ground or in low bushes.

Page 44

1. Marsh Warbler; it doesn't arrive until May, when Peregrines will have hatched. It is anyway a rarity in Wales. It is more likely to have been a Reed Warbler. *2.* Nightjar; which also arrives in May and could not have been heard at that time. *3.* Golden Eagle; it may have bred in Wales at one time but it has become a rare vagrant. Twitchett is most likely to have seen a Buzzard.

Pages 45-47

1. Rock Dove. *2.* Kittiwake. *3.* Bittern. *4.* None that you can see. Only the male sings. *5.* Eagle. *6.* Eclipse. *7.* Sir Peter Scott. *8.* Cormorant. *9.* Blackcap. *10.* Fieldfare and Redwing. *11.* Mute Swan. *12.* Red Kite. *13.* Hobby. *14.* Scottish Crossbill. *15.* Black-tailed Godwit. *16.* Skuas. *17.* White Wagtail. *18.* Turtle Dove. *19.* Eider. *20.* Ring-necked (or Rose-ringed) Parakeet. *21.* Albatross. *22.* Goldeneye, Golden Plover, Golden Eagle, Golden Pheasant, Golden Oriole. *23.* Ring Ousel. *24.* Avocet. *25.* Mandarin Duck. *26.* Brambling. *27.* Cuckoo. *28.* Swallow. *29.* Bearded Tit. *30.* Ptarmigan. *31.* Nightjar. *32.* Nuthatch. *33.* Eleonora. *34.* Velvet Scoter. *35.* Eagle Owl. *36.* Tawny Owl. *37.* Scaup. *38.* Brent Goose. *39.* Magpie. *40.* Woodcock. *41.* Swallow. *42.* Hedge Sparrow, or Hedge Accentor. *43.* Yellow Wagtail. *44.* House Martin. *45.* Chaffinch. *46.* Firecrest. *47.* Coal Tit. *48.* Yellowhammer. *49.* The

Lake District. *50.* Sea cliffs. *51.* In roof spaces. *52.* In the wing. *53.* Mallard. *54.* The male has a thicker black stripe down its belly. *55.* Bullfinch. *56.* Redshank has white in the wing. *57.* Mistle Thrush. *58.* Redwing. *59.* The Song Thrush repeats its phrases, the Blackbird doesn't. *60.* Black Redstart. *61.* Redshank. *62.* Pied Wagtail, Pied Flycatcher, Magpie. *63.* Common Tern. *64.* Great Black-backed Gull.

Page 49

The unlikely, or erroneous, observations are: *1.* The Willow Warbler's anxiety note is *di*syllabic: this was a Chiffchaff. *2.* This is the wrong habitat for a Meadow Pipit: it was a Tree Pipit. *3.* Brambling are not in England during July: these were presumably more Chaffinches. *4.* Male and female Hobby are indistinguishable. *5.* The description of the Wryneck's call is wrong (and the Wryneck is anyway very unlikely): this was a Lesser Spotted Woodpecker. *6.* The drawing shows a Skylark, not a Woodlark.

Pages 50-53

1. Veery, Yellow Warbler, Cape May Warbler, Hooded Warbler, Magnolia Warbler, Summer Tanager, Fox Sparrow, Rufous-sided Towhee, Savannah Sparrow, Brown Thrasher, Cliff Swallow, Philadelphia Vireo and Catbird. *2.* American Bittern, Coot, Purple Gallinule, Kestrel, Pipit, Redstart, Robin, Wigeon. *3.* Red-necked Grebe, Black-necked Grebe, Ring-necked Duck, Red-necked Stint, Red-necked Phalarope, Ring-necked Parakeet. *4.* Red-breasted Goose, Red-breasted Merganser, Buff-breasted Sandpiper, Red-breasted Flycatcher, Rose-breasted Grosbeak, Yellow-breasted Bunting. *5.* White-billed Diver, Pied-billed Grebe, Broad-billed Sandpiper, Long-billed Dowitcher, Short-billed Dowitcher, Ring-billed Gull, Slender-billed Gull, Gull-billed Tern, Yellow-billed Cuckoo, Black-billed Cuckoo, Thick-billed Warbler. *6.* Long-tailed Duck, White-tailed Eagle, Bar-tailed Godwit, Black-tailed Godwit, White-tailed Plover, Sharp-tailed Sandpiper, Long-tailed Skua,

Needle-tailed Swift, Long-tailed Tit, Fan-tailed Warbler. 7. Common, Alpine, Chimney, Little, Needle-tailed, Pacific, Pallid. 8. Aleutian, Arctic, Black, Bridled, Caspian, Common, Forster's, Gull-billed, Little, Roseate, Royal, Sandwich, Sooty, Whiskered, White-winged, Black. (At the time of writing Lesser Crested and Elegant Terns are still under consideration). 9. Reed, Yellow(hammer), Black-headed, Cirl, Corn, Cretzschmar's, Lapland, Little, Ortolan, Pallas's Reed, Pine, Rock, Rustic, Snow, Yellow-breasted, Yellow-browed. 10. Bittern, American Bittern, Little Bittern, Cattle Egret, Little Egret, Great White Egret, Green Heron, Grey Heron, Night Heron, Purple Heron, Squacco Heron. 11. Green, Marmora's. 12. 1889. 13. Black Duck. 14. Thick-billed Warbler. 15. Bass Rock. 16. They were all once rarities but have now been removed from the BBRC list. 17. They are white in Swallow, black in Red-rumped. 18. Grey-cheeked Thrush. It is not a member of the genus *Turdus*. 19. Sardinian, Orphean, Desert, Ruppell's, Marmora's. 20. Great Snipe, Wilson's Phalarope, Baird's Sandpiper, Broad-billed Sandpiper, Marsh Sandpiper. 21. Cory's Shearwater. 22. Houbara Bustard. 23. It has no black mask. 24. Hudsonian Godwit. 25. They are all Hastings rarities. 26. Kenfig Pool. 27. Brown Thrasher. 28. Slate-coloured Junco, Co. Clare 1905. 29. Long-billed Dowitcher, 1801. 30. Black Kite, White-tailed Eagle, Pallid Harrier, Gyrfalcon, Lesser Kestrel, American Kestrel, Red-footed Falcon, Eleonora's Falcon. 31. Solitary Sandpiper does not have a white rump. 32. Pallas's Grasshopper Warbler has white tips to its tail feathers. 33. Cape May Warbler. 34. Yellow Warbler. 35. White-winged Lark. 36. Long-toed Stint. 37. To see a Lesser White-fronted Goose. 38. Bufflehead, Hooded Merganser. 39. Lesser Short-toed Lark. 40. Seven to date: Common, Black, Black-eared, Desert, Isabelline, Pied, White-crowned Black. 41. Moustached Warbler. 42. Nutcrackers. 43. American race has no white rump. 44. Black-winged Stilt. 45. Bee-eater. 46. Brown. 47. Penduline Tit. 48. Spotted Sandpiper. 49. Black-and-white Warbler. 50. Yellow-bellied Sapsucker. 51. Sheathbill. 52. Juveniles have black wing-tips, adults don't. 53. Little Gull. 54. Mew Gull. 55. Canada Goose, Egyptian Goose, Ruddy Duck, Mandarin, Red-legged Partridge, Pheasant, Golden Pheasant, Lady Amherst's Pheasant, Capercaillie, Ring-necked Parakeet, Little Owl. 56. Pechora Pipit. 57. 6: Bonaparte's, Franklin's, Great Black-headed, Laughing, Little, Mediterranean. (Black-headed has a brown head, Sabine's a grey head). 58. Lundy. 59. Ortolan, Little, Rustic, Yellow-breasted, Black-headed. 60. Black-eared, Desert, Pied, Black, Isabelline. 61. Rock Pipit, Water Pipit and American Pipit. 62. White-tailed Plover. 63. Sandhill Crane. 64. Trumpeter Finch.

Page 62

1. Warblers which occur in the autumn as vagrants from Siberia. *2.* The immature Blue-headed Wagtail was more likely to be a Yellow Wagtail, but the two races are indistinguishable in immature plumage anyway. *3.* The only wader likely to be confused with a Pectoral Sandpiper is the rarer Sharp-tailed Sandpiper from Siberia.

Pages 63-65

1. Bit-tern. *2.* B-rambling. *3.* Buzz-'ard. *4.* Razor-bill. *5.* Night-ingale. *6.* Kitti-wake. *7.* Si-skin. *8.* Roller. *9.* Swallow. *10.* Bee-eater. *11.* Moor-hen. *12.* Whim-br-el. *13.* Dipper. *14.* Hobby. *15.* Sand Martin. *16.* Wil(l)-son's Petrel. *17.* Black Kite. *18.* Chough. *19.* House Sparrow. *20.* Jay. *21.* Golden-eye. *22.* Gad-wall. *23.* Greens-hank. *24.* Chaff-inch. *25.* Harle(y)-quin. *26.* Turtle Dove. *27.* Dun-lin. *28.* Stone-chat. *29.* Po-marine Skua. *30.* Velvet Scot-er. *31.* Snip-e. *32.* Wax-wing. *33.* Sanderling. *34.* Mandarin. *35.* Blue-throat. *36.* Capercaillie. *37.* Sabine's Gull. *38.* Green Sandpiper. *39.* Tree Pipit. *40.* Grey Phalarope. *41.* Nightingale. *42.* Fieldfare. *43.* Collared Dove. *44.* Corncrake. *45.* Red Grouse. *46.* Roseate Tern. *47.* Oystercatcher. *48.* Storm Petrel. *49.* Short-eared Owl. *50.* Great Skua. *51.* Little Grebe. *52.* House Martin. *53.* Water rail. *54.* Reed Bunting. *55.* Shore Lark. *56.* Manx Shearwater. *57.* Spotted Fly-catcher. *58.* Red-throated Diver. *59.* Bearded Tit. *60.* Garganey. *61.* Garden Warbler. *62.* Great Grey Shrike. *63.* Turnstone. *64.* Ringed Plover.

Page 68

The two errors that Mr Duesbury presumably pointed out are: *1.* The Coot in the illustration is an American Coot, distinguished by its dark tipped bill. *2.* The Smew in the background would not be seen together with the Corncrake: the Smew is a winter visitor, the Corncrake a summer one.

Pages 72-74

1. Treecreeper. *2*. Grey Phalarope. *3*. Chough. *4*. Collared Dove. *5*. Mute Swan. *6*. Water Rail. *7*. Dotterel. *8*. Jack Snipe. *9*. Arctic Tern. *10*. Skylark. *11*. Peregrine. *12*. Great Spotted Woodpecker. *13*. Corn Bunting. *14*. Bittern. *15*. Swallow. *16*. Pied Wagtail. *17*. Little Stint. *18*. Puffin. *19*. Nuthatch. *20*. Black-headed Gull. *21*. Green Woodpecker. *22*. Redstart. *23*. Barn Owl. *24*. Common Scoter. *25*. Coot. *26*. Raven. *27*. Wren. *28*. Nutcracker. *29*. Siskin. *30*. Dipper. *31*. Woodcock. *32*. Cuckoo. *33*. Corncrake. *34*. Long-tailed Tit. *35*. Manx Shearwater. *36*. Starling. *37*. Snow Goose. *38*. Whimbrel. *39*. Wigeon. *40*. Little Grebe. *41*. Honey Buzzard. *42*. Gannet. *43*. Great Skua. *44*. Red Grouse. *45*. Lapwing. *46*. Knot. *47*. Sanderling. *48*. Pheasant. *49*. Tree Sparrow. *50*. Merlin. *51*. House Martin. *52*. Song Thrush. *53*. Ruff. *54*. Tawny Owl. *55*. Grey Heron. *56*. Ptarmigan. *57*. Ringed Plover. *58*. Rock Dove. *59*. Sandwich Tern. *60*. Little Owl. *61*. Shag. *62*. Snipe. *63*. Swift. *64*. Sand Martin.

Page 79

1. Downy Woodpecker, an American species which is resident and therefore unlikely to stray over here. *2*. The photo of the Whiskered Tern diving, since they feed on insects and not fish.

Page 81

The four mistakes are: *1*. The drawing is of an immature Lesser Black-backed Gull, not a Herring Gull. *2*. Jack Snipe neither zig-zag nor tower: this was a Snipe. *3*. A Rock Pipit is unlikely: it was probably a Meadow Pipit on the beach. *4*. The drawing is of an immature Sedge Warbler, not an Aquatic Warbler.

Pages 82-84

1. South Africa. *2.* Australia. *3.* Kiwis. *4.* Cowbirds. *5.* Madagascar. *6.* New Zealand. *7.* Birds of Paradise. *8.* Pheasants and Partridges. *9.* Peacock or Blue Peafowl. *10.* Turkey. *11.* Madagascar, Mauritius and the Seychelles. *12.* West Indies. *13.* Sunbirds. *14.* Toucans. *15.* Short-toed Eagle. *16.* Amsterdam Island. *17.* North, Central and South America. *18.* Madagascar. *19.* Storm Petrel. *20.* Emperor Penguin. *21.* Cardinal. *22.* Magnificent Frigatebird. *23.* India and Sri Lanka. *24.* Africa. *25.* Bird of Paradise. *26.* Pheasant. *27.* Australia. *28.* A finch. *29.* South America. *30.* Australia. *31.* Kabylie Nuthatch. *32.* Canary Island Chat. *33.* Storks. *34.* The Swallow. *35.* South America. *36.* Gibraltar. *37.* Horned, Tufted and Atlantic. *38.* Prunellidae or accentors. *39.* Social Weaver. *40.* They are all the only members of their respective wader families. *41.* Australia. *42.* Bali. *43.* Fiery throated Awlbill – a type of hummingbird. *44.* Kingfishers. *45.* Diving Petrels. *46.* They are all named after mountains — Andean Condor, Alpine Swift and Himalayan Rubythroat. *47.* New Caledonia. *48.* New Zealand. *49.* *Otis* is a bustard, *Otus* is an owl. *50.* *Crex* is a corncrake, *Crax* is a curassow. *51.* Atlantic Ocean. It is the Wilson's Petrel. *52.* Japan, also China and Korea. It is the Japanese Crested Ibis. *53.* Hawaii. *54.* Madagascar. *55.* Crane. *56.* Falconiformes, which includes all bird of prey. *57.* Red-necked Phalarope, Grey Phalarope, Dotterel and Andalusian Hemipode. *58.* Hawaii. *59.* Central and South America. *60.* Galapagos. *61.* It takes place in a specially built garden, decorated with coloured stones and flowers. *62.* They can climb with claws on their wings and can swim well. *63.* Megapodes or Mallee Fowl. *64.* Emperor Penguin.

Page 93

1. He stated that the hovering falcon must be a Kestrel, but Redfooted Falcons also hover. *2.* A Cuckoo. *3.* A Sooty Shearwater if it was dark phase, or a Great Shearwater if it was pale phase. *4.* Assuming the oil had blackened its belly, he would have mistaken it for a Black Tern. *5.* A Dunnock.

Pages 94-97

1. All are vagrants to Great Britain from America. *2.* All are introduced to Briatin and now breed without assistance. *3.* All will eat the young of other birds. *4.* The scientific generic and specific names are the same in each case. *5.* The parents all leave their young before they fledge. *6.* All are known commonly by other names in Britain. *7.* All were thought to be extinct, but were then rediscovered. *8.* All are flightless. *9.* All nest in holes in trees. *10.* All nest in holes in the ground. *11.* All have webbed feet. *12.* All have forked tails. *13.* All are colonial nesters. *14.* All can be prefixed 'Wood'. *15.* All have, or appear to have, upturned bills. *16.* They are all the only representatives of their families in Europe. *17.* All the adult males have a black mask across the eye. *18.* All eat carrion. *19.* They all have a diagnostic eye-stripe. *20.* They are all named after vegetation. *21.* They are all named after their food. *22.* They are all named for the sound they make. *23.* All have distinctive forehead patches. *24.* All have red on their heads in summer. *25.* All the names are misleading or spurious in some way. *26.* All normally nest in coniferous woodland. *27.* All are named for some aspect of their behaviour. *28.* All are named after other species. *29.* All have different colour phases. *30.* All can be prefixed with a person's name to give a rarer species – Steller, Blyth and Pallas. *31.* Their second names can be replaced by 'Warbler'. *32.* Their first names can all be replaced by 'Spotted'. *33.* Reed Bunting: it is the only one that doesn't nest in reeds. *34.* Gadwall: it has no relations whose names are made by adding a prefix to its own. *35.* Ptarmigan: it is the only one to stay in montane habitats all year round. *36.* Lesser Whitethroat: the sexes are similar. The others all show differences between males and females. *37.* Black-billed Cuckoo: it is the only one that is not a brood parasite. *38.* Glaucous Gull: it is the only that breeds exclusively on coasts. *39.* Great Crested Grebe: it is the only monogamous species. *40.* Honey Buzzard: it belongs to the genus *Pernis*; the others are all genus *Buteo*. *41.* Collared Dove: it never nests colonially. *42.* Spotted Flycatcher: it moults its wing from the outside primaries inwards. *43.* Grey Partridge: it is the only one without red legs, and it is in the genus *Perdix* rather than *Alectoris*. *44.* Little Crake: the sexes differ; in the others, they are similar. *45.* Grey Heron: unlike the others, it will nest on the ground. *46.* White-tailed Eagle was once a native species; the others are all alien introductions. *47.* Robin: it is the only one without white in the wing in flight. *48.* Black Kite: it is the only one never to have bred in Britain. *49.* Goldfinch: the sexes are similar, in the the others they are different. *50.* Gannet: it dives from the air, the others from the water. *51.* Kittiwake: it only flocks in the breeding season. *52.* Blackcap: the female does not have a black cap, the other females do. *53.* Osprey: it is the only one whose family is monospecific. *54.* Kingfisher: it is the only one whose rump is not white. *55.* Kingfisher: it is the only one that does not vary geographically. *56.* Avocet: it is the only one whose scientific specific name is not *alba*. *57.* Great Skua: it is the only species without a corresponding 'Lesser'. *58.* Red-legged Partridge: in the other species, the name applies only to the male's plumage. *59.* Black-tailed Godwit: the other species are named after only their seasonal plumage. *60.* Great Crested Grebe: it is the only one whose name can't be converted to the name of another species by removal of the word Great. *61.* White-throated Sparrow: it is a Bunting, while the others are all sparrows. *62.* White Stork: it is the only one whose name cannot be prefixed by Grey. *63.* Blue Tit: it is the only true tit (belonging to the genus *Parus*). *64.* Golden Eagle: it is the only one that doesn't breed in Ireland.

Page 99

The five errors are: *1.* The drawing is of a young Arctic, not a Long-tailed, Skua. *2.* Little Auks fly low over the waves in tight flocks and level flight, and wouldn't be in the Channel in September anyway. *3.* Crested Larks stay where they are; they don't approach England. *4.* The drawing is of a juvenile Kittiwake, not a Sabine's Gull. *5.* The drawing is of a juvenile Arctic Tern, not a Common Tern.

Page 104

1. The Purple Sandpiper at Cliffe. Purple Sandpipers spend the winter on rocky coasts and would not be seen in spring on the North Kent marshes. *2.* The Savi's Warbler. Savi's Warblers tend not to perch in bushes and are lower, not slower, than a Grasshopper Warbler (which the bird must have been). *3.* The White-rumped Sandpiper. Curlew Sandpipers have a white rump and a white wing stripe which White-rumped lacks. *4.* Although the Capercaillie was a native British Bird, it became extinct in in the 17th century. It was introduced back in the mid-18th century and so would not be counted by a birder with a 'pure' list.

Pages 105-107

1. Wren. *2.* Cetti's Warbler. *3.* Snow Bunting. *4.* Wilson's Petrel and Great Skua have been recorded at the South Pole. *5.* Fan-tailed Warbler. *6.* Common Sandpiper. *7.* Oystercatcher and Ringed Plover, on the Isles of Scilly. *8.* Twite, on Shetland. *9.* Magpie. *10.* Green Woodpecker. *11.* Reedbeds. *12.* Upland moorland. *13.* They show no white in the wing. *14.* Temminck's Stint. *15.* Swallow, House Martin and Sand Martin. *16.* Black Guillemot, Guillemot, Puffin, Razorbill. *17.* Red-breasted Merganser. *18.* Sandwich Tern. *19.* Eider. *20.* Shoveler. *21.* Shore Lark. *22.* Lapland Bunting. *23.* Blackbird, on Shetland. *24.* Sedge Warbler on Orkney. *25.* Grasshopper Warbler. *26.* Firecrest. *27.* South Africa. *28.* The Sahel region, south of the Sahara. *29.* To attract a mate. *30.* As a defence mechanism. *31.* Oak. It buries acorns to store them. *32.* It impales it on a thorn to form a 'larder'. *33.* Nutcracker. *34.* Honey Buzzard. *35.* Spurn Point. *36.* Portland Bill. *37.* A fine 'invisible' net with pockets to trap birds which fly into it. Used to catch birds for ringing. *38.* Golden-yellow tufts of feathers behind the eye. *39.* Chestnut-red head and underparts. *40.* A funnel-shaped wire netting cage with bushes and trees at its mouth into which birds can be driven. Used to catch birds for ringing. *41.* To distract a predator away from its nest or young. *42.* It thinks that its reflection in the hub-cap is a rival. *43.* Fulmar. *44.* Wood Pigeon. *45.* Six. Three on each foot. *46.* Eight. Four on each foot. *47.* One. *48.* Three or four. *49.* In reedbeds. *50.* In flight. *51.* Purple Heron. *52.* Turtle Dove. *53.* Pine needles. *54.* By dropping them from the air onto hard ground. *55.* Yes, especially when holding food. *56.* No, although nocturnal birds may have little or no colour vision. *57.* To stir up food particles. *58.* Because it uses its tail to balance when climbing up or along and couldn't balance when climbing down. *59.* No. They will sing from the ground or from a perch. *60.* Yes, if it was flying. Their wings make a whistling noise. The birds will also snort and hiss when disturbed. *61.* Mallard. *62.* Blackbird. *63.* Longtailed Duck. *64.* House Martin.

Page 114

1. It would have been regarded as an escape, as they are kept in captivity in Britain. *2.* Sardinian Warblers do not occur in northern France, except as vagrants. *3.* Garganey, as it migrates to Africa, not western Europe.